AF526203

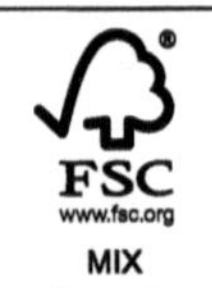
FSC
www.fsc.org
MIX
Papper från ansvarsfulla källor
Paper from responsible sources
FSC® C105338

PHD PROJECT

PEDAGOGIES OF THE UNKNOWN

– studying for a future, without guarantees

Lisa Nyberg
Doctor of Philosophy (PhD)

Vienna, November 2021
Registration number: r1470126
Study Number/Studienblatt: UR 094 607 Doctor of Philosophy in Practice
Field of Study/Studienblatt: Art Theory and Cultural Studies
Supervisors: Prof. Dr. Anette Baldauf, Prof. Dr. Renate Lorenz

Graphic design: Jan Petterson, janpetterson.se
Photography: Lisa Nyberg, Terje Östling, Keiko Uenishi
Fonts: Tisa Pro & Horseferry
ISBN: 978-91-8027-690-0
Förlag: BoD – Books on Demand, Stockholm, Sverige
Tryck: BoD – Books on Demand, Norderstedt, Tyskland

ASTRACT ENGLISH

THIS PHD PROJECT STARTS FROM THE QUESTION: *how can we study for a future unknown?* In light of anthropogenic climate change, a global environmental crisis, and its destabilizing impact on social and economic systems, there is an urgency to examine how we relate to the future in our pedagogy; how we anticipate, imagine and prepare through our teaching and our studies. In the search of pedagogies that are open to not knowing – to contingency, unpredictability and change – the question arises: what could a pedagogy look like that supports our studies with and for the unknown?

At the basis of this research is a teaching practice; the classroom of aesthetic education at the intersection of study, creative work and the institution. From this base a performance practice has developed that draws from lecture performance and meditation as a quotidian and creative practice, to create a series of guided meditations. These are presented as art installations, as sound pieces and as activities in the classroom. The guided meditations propose an experiment in how to address the contradiction of learning for the future, by focusing, intently, on the present.

This project attempts to interrupt the linearity of critical consciousness theory by displacing Paulo Freire's concept *conscientização*, or critical consciousness, from its place at the pinnacle of a linear telling of empowerment, to a place where it is intersecting with other forms of consciousness. Simultaneously, the project raises a critique of Western constructs of utopia as the dominant form of imagining otherwise, by looking to feminist and de-colonial theory that resist utopian fatalism and claims to universality. The aim is to make a critical shift from utopia towards a constantly changing and undetermined future – the unknown.

ABSTRACT GERMAN

DAS VORLIEGENDE PHD-PROJEKT nimmt seinen Ausgang in der Frage: *Wie für eine ungewisse Zukunft lernen?* In Anbetracht des von Menschen verursachten Klimawandels, einer globalen Umweltkrise und deren destabilisierenden Auswirkungen auf soziale und ökonomische Systeme ergibt sich eine Dringlichkeit uns damit auseinanderzusetzen, wie wir durch unsere Pädagogik mit der Zukunft in Beziehung treten; wie wir diese voraussehen, imaginieren und uns durch unser Lehren und Lernen auf sie vorbereiten. Auf der Suche nach Pädagogiken, die sich dem Nichtwissen öffnen – der Zufälligkeit, Unvorhersehbarkeit und dem Wandel – stellt sich die Frage, wie eine Pädagogik aussehen kann, welche unsere Auseinandersetzung mit und auf das *Ungewisse* ausgerichtet, zu unterstützen und fördern vermag.

Die Grundlage dieser Forschung bildet die Praxis des Lehrens; der Klassenraum ästhetischer Bildung an der Schnittstelle von Studium, kreativer Arbeit und Institution. Darauf aufbauend, und Bezug nehmend auf die Formate der Lecture Performance und der Meditation als alltägliche und kreative Praktiken, hat sich eine performative Praxis entwickelt, welche in der Herausbildung einer Reihe von geführten Meditationen mündete. Diese werden als Installationen, als Klangkunst und als Aktivitäten im Unterricht präsentiert. Die geführten Meditationen schlagen ein Experiment vor: Wie die Widersprüche angehen, die sich daraus ergeben, dass wir für die Zukunft lernen, indem wir uns mit aller Aufmerksamkeit auf die Gegenwart konzentrieren?

Dieses Projekt unternimmt den Versuch die Linearität der Kritischen Theorie zu durchbrechen, indem es Paulo Freires Konzept des kritischen Bewusstseins (por. *conscientização*) von seinem Platz an der Spitze einer linearen Vorstellung von Empowerment an einen Ort verlagert, an dem es mit anderen Konzeptionen von Bewusstsein in Beziehung tritt. Zumal feministische und dekoloniale Theorien herangezogen werden, die sich utopischem Fatalismus und Behauptungen von Universalität entgegenstellen, übt die vorliegende Untersuchung somit gleichzeitig Kritik an westlichen Konstrukten der Utopie als dominanter Form des Imaginierens eines *Anderenfalls*. Das Ziel ist eine entscheidende Verschiebung: weg von der Utopie hin zu einer Vorstellung einer sich konstant verändernden und unbestimmten Zukunft – dem *Ungewissen*.

BIOGRAPHY

LISA NYBERG IS A VISUAL ARTIST BASED IN MALMÖ, SWEDEN. She explores the radical possibilities of pedagogy and performance through processes that involve collective, embodied, transgressive and critical practices. In her work, she examines cultural and educational canons from an intersectional feminist perspective. This means creating situations and structures where learning can take place, as well as intervening in existing structures and institutions. Nyberg's work takes the form of self-organized spaces, institutional processes, workshops, performances, installations, books and sound pieces.

Nyberg was one of the founders of Malmö Free University for Women (2006–2011) and the think tank on Radical Pedagogy (2011–2014), as well as the network X-front (2007–2010). Since 2015 she is part of UNICORN – artists in solidarity, an organization that explores forms of solidarity between artists through the sharing of food, experiences, knowledge and by organizing a residency for artists at risk. In 2016–2017 Nyberg was the head teacher and coordinator of Malmö Konstverkstad, and in 2019–2020 she was Head of Studies for The School of Conceptual and Contextual Practices at The Royal Danish Academy of Fine Arts.

Lisa Nyberg's work has been exhibited at Kunsthal Aarhus, the Research Pavilion at the Venice Biennale, Konsthall C (Stockholm), Trondheim Art Biennial, Signal–Center for Contemporary Art (Malmö), Röda Sten (Gothenburg), Den Frie Udstillingsbygning (Copenhagen), Dunkers Kulturhus (Helsingborg), Liljevalchs Konsthall (Stockholm), Gothenburg Art Museum, Rooseum (Malmö) among others. She has been awarded two working grants from the Swedish Arts Grants Committee as well as the Malmö City Grant for Artistic Development. Nyberg teaches regularly at art academies in the Nordic countries, such as The Royal Danish Academy of Fine Arts, The Danish National School of Performing Arts, Konstfack, Valand Art Academy, Malmö University and others.

www.lisanyberg.net

TABLE OF CONTENTS

DOCUMENTATION

ACKNOWLEDGEMENTS

This dissertation would not have come about without the support from my fellow candidates at the PhD-in-Practice program in Vienna: thank you Hong-Kai Wang for the long talks and good food, Anna T for generously sharing facts and fun, Belinda Kazeem-Kamiński for telling truths and reminding me of what I have to offer. Thanks to my generation buddies – Rafal Morusiewicz, Hristina Ivanoska and Janine Jembere, who started this journey with me.

Thank you to my supervisors, Anette Baldauf and Renate Lorenz, who accepted my reluctant ass to the program and carried me through.

Thank you Julia Giertz for the warm guidance into the world of sound.

Thank you to my critical friends: Adriana Seserin – enthusiastic reader and gracious language devotee, Kristina Lindström – my guide to academic life (and life), Stina Nyberg – astonished contemplator and playmate.

Thank you to the people who have trusted me to be their teacher, especially at Malmö Konstverkstad, Billedkunstskolerne/ Det Kongelige Danske Kunstakademi and Scenekunstskolen in Copenhagen and Aarhus – I have learned so much from studying with you.

Thank you Erich Koller who welcomed me to Vienna and offered me a place to stay.

Thank you Helge Ax:son Johnsons stiftelse for covering my travel costs.

Thank you friends who believed in me and irritated me with your questions and anticipation. I hope you will not be disappointed.

Thank you mamma, pappa and systrarna for reminding me that life comes first.

Thank you EvaMarie Lindahl, my academic wife and the only one who really knows every turn on this journey. You caught my tears, validated my worries, snapped me out of self-doubt and mirrored my brilliance in yours.

Thank you Sten Nyberg and Terje Östling, the nucleus of my life.

THE CLASSROOM

LET ME CARVE OUT THIS SPACE FOR US. Let me furnish this dissertation as a classroom – a place of study. We will need an element of curiosity, an element of trust, an element of risk. We will need a place to gather, with some space to think, to sit and to move around. I will ask you to bring your bags, your bodies, your attention, your pens and paper, your water. I will provide material for us to engage with. I will bring in concepts and ideas we can hold in our hands; to touch and smell, poke with our fingers, remould to fit our hands and to stretch out between us in threads and blankets. I will bring in guest teachers; the voices of Paulo Freire, Gayatri Chakravorty Spivak, Vanessa de Oliveira Andreotti, Gloria Anzaldúa and others. I will set up experiments in the form of guided meditations, to see what they make possible in terms of study. I will bring my experience, from teaching and from my art practice, as I hope you will bring yours.

This classroom is intended for those who are working in the intersection of art and pedagogy; artists who teach, teachers who use art in their teaching, artists who see the pedagogy of their artworks, teachers who think like artists, teachers who are performers, performance artists who teach, art teachers at institutions and activists who use art to come together to study.

My longing to be with you has led me to invite you to this classroom, to study together. Invitation to this "we" might leave you uncomfortable – you might need to refuse, to resist, to claim your independence and stand on the sideline to just listen in. You might not be able to join at this point. You might not trust me yet, and maybe you shouldn't. I will keep inviting you, though.

Let me offer a series of definitions of "we" that you may feel implicated in, comfortable with, challenged by or longing for:

– We who have the privilege to walk in and out of educational institutions and art spaces to do our practice, however ill or well defined. We who have places to come together with others. We who have the space and time to do art, to teach, who have platforms and words to speak our truth (sometimes in a whisper). We who have people who will listen.

– We who have fought ourselves in from the margins, and keep on struggling to stay connected to where we came from. We who embody the dreams of our ancestors and carry this responsibility in our hearts. We who often wonder why we dreamt of this place in the first place and doubt what is possible here.

– We who try to transgress the borders of education and the walls of institutions. We who spatter paint on the white walls and leave traces of mud on the floors. We who turn the gaze to the space, the institution and its structures, tearing at the wallpapers to find what is beneath. We who organize every space, attempting to build communities and foster relations that cut through hierarchies. We who drop seeds that sprout long after we are gone.

– We who see teaching as relational work. We who study as we teach.

– We who gather in circles around tables or on the floor, to think together with others and try to understand the world. We who study in activist and community spaces. We who dig where we stand in a collective effort, and face the pain of what is unearthed together.

– We who search for ways of teaching beyond what we already know of educational, institutional and pedagogical structures. We who search for radical pedagogies that help us teach without a goal; to teach what cannot be measured, weighed, valued; to teach at the edge of what we know.

– We who are unsettled by these catastrophic times and search for ways to deal with the unknown. We who have a sense that what we have done so far is not enough. We who are convinced of the incapability of imperialist heterosexist global capitalism to handle this future. We who fear the pervasiveness of universalist logics, simple solutions and fascist conclusions. We who work to imagine otherwise.

I would like to be precise in how I configure the urgency of our studies together. When entering this classroom in 2021, our lives are imbued with an acute sense of unpredictability. The global pandemic has brought our societies' spinning wheels to a halt, forcing us to slow down, to physically separate and isolate. People around me are losing loved ones, their health, their jobs, their sanity and safety. Simultaneously, on a planetary timescale, the acceleration of natural disasters is ongoing. The number of heat waves, storms and wild fires are breaking records every other year. Indigenous activists are screaming from the top of their lungs for all to hear, scientists are working to get their data published in mainstream media, and school kids are gathering every Friday to protest. In the background, the silence grows from populations of species going extinct and echoes from scanty forests and paling sea beds.

The urgent threat of climate change is not simply that it will kill us all – I fear our reaction in the face of the unknown. A threat rises from how the response to climate catastrophe is formulated; with claims to universality, of humanity as a homogeneous entity that faces an outer threat; claims that ignore the immense difference in whose lives are valued and protected by the current systems, and whose lives are not. It is not "humanity" that has brought on this catastrophe – it is specific systems and cultures (namely predatory capitalism, different forms of colonization and neo-liberal rationalization). Similarly, it is not humanity that needs to be protected. This logic could entail the sacrifice of less valued life for the benefit of the greater good, i.e. to let parts of the world's population die so that humanity as an entity can live on. It leads to arguments where the seemingly rational erases the individual, and lives become numbers that fall off the scale. The urgency of catastrophic times paves way for fascist solutions, unless we imagine otherwise.

It is important here to recognize that for the displaced, dispossessed or oppressed, the present is already catastrophic. Many live with futures that are constantly under threat. This means that there is already plenty of experience of dealing with catastrophic times, destabilized presents and unknown futures. In this classroom we will listen to those with experience, those who have been here many times before – native and black intellectuals, post- and decolonial thinkers, queer and crip organizers, to name a few. People with the specific knowledge that rises from forming resistance to the large scale, systematic obstructions to a liveable future, and the experience of a life without guarantees.

In this classroom, we will respond to the urgency of the unknown by practising our skills for dealing with uncertainty, paying attention and imagining otherwise. Additionally, our work will need to extend beyond our classroom. What we understand and practice in this room needs to be implemented and lead to action, outside. We need to find ways to translate our philosophies to politics, to strengthen our communities and share our resources in ways that hold space for more than ourselves. We need to organize together with others and join the movements that are already in operation. The bravery we gather in here, needs to accelerate out there. I wish for our studies in this classroom to transgress these walls.

METHODOLOGY

THE PHD PROJECT *Pedagogies of the Unknown* starts from the question: how can we study for a future unknown? In teaching, there is always this question of what we are teaching for: how what we teach is relevant to the lives of the students and their future, as well as to our professional field, or even to society as a whole. How can we teach when we do not know what we are teaching for? To students, in different forms of study, the corresponding question becomes: how can we study for a future unknown? To better understand these questions, I have looked into the different ways we relate to the future through pedagogy: how we anticipate and prepare for the future, in and beyond education. What kind of pedagogies can support our studies with and for the unknown?

A critical aspect of this inquiry is to think about how we can imagine otherwise, beyond what current dominating systems teach us about the future. How can we imagine beyond colonial, nationalist, universalist and capitalist logic? To imagine otherwise, our practices of imagining will need to change – it is not only about *what*, but also about *how* we imagine. In this project I have attempted to explore how we can engage all our senses in the service of studying for the unknown, with all the different facets of our consciousness. What could a radical pedagogy look like, that take into consideration all that we have in our power to imagine otherwise?

These questions are investigated through a practice-based research. My experience from art and teaching forms the undercurrent, the stream from where questions and ideas rise to the surface. These questions and ideas are gathered in an experiment, exploring how guided meditations can function as a pedagogical practice. From this experiment new questions and ideas detach, floating freely, before slowly sinking back down to join the undercurrent.

This stream will take us on a journey, from the search for a radical pedagogy, to the experiment with guided meditations, through a reflection on the experiences and ideas that can be deducted from those experiments, and a discussion on the possibilities and contradictions informed by the focus on critical consciousness in radical pedagogy. We end with practice and a place to start: a guided meditation for the unknown at the heart of our lives.

If you prefer to start with the practice, you can find the manuscripts to the guided meditations, with short introductions and links to sound files, at the end of this document. You can also do the guided meditation called *Induction: An unknown at the heart of our lives* that you find as the last chapter of this dissertation.

My experience of teaching comes from teaching adults at different stages on their path to art, with different backgrounds, and in varied forms of institutions. I teach in art academies of both fine arts and performing arts, mainly as a guest teacher or as a visiting professor. I also teach fine arts in adult education at a pre-university level, and I am often invited to do workshops in art institutions, such as galleries and museums, as well as in self-organized spaces. I have been involved in art education initiatives involving collaborations between schools and museums, aimed at expanding access to the art world for people not generally represented in the art academies, galleries or museums.

My artistic practice takes the form of performances and installations, self-organized spaces, institutional processes, workshops, sound pieces and printed matter. I started out as a sculptor by training, but moved towards more installation and performance based practices, inspired by feminist artists from previous generations. Most of my work is done in collaboration with others, and I am continuously engaged in different collectives. In 2006 Johanna Gustavsson and me started the Malmö Free University for Women (MFK), and later we proceeded to work with a think tank on radical pedagogy. This collaboration has inspired a lot of my later work.

My teaching and my artistic practice are interrelated and inform one another. I am interested in the pedagogy of both art and education – how we learn through the encounter with and the making of art, the pedagogy of the art work, and how it induces change – and I am driven by this search for a radical pedagogy. *Pedagogy* is a word not easily translated; in some languages it is closely connected to education, in others to the formal upbringing of children, in some it is more in the realms of teaching methods. The latter is how I will use the term in this project – pedagogy as in how we structure situations of study, followed closely by *why* we structure our studies as we do. I have used pedagogy as a way of thinking across the different areas of my practice, whether it be installations, performances, writing or teaching, and to look for radical ways to structure the situation, to invite the audience/participant/student into the conversation and incite the urge to study.[1] Reflecting on my practice, I have found it necessary to question some of the radical possibilities of pedagogy, to recognize its presumptions and limitations, and ventured out into the unknown.

To study is the intellectual activities we do every day to understand the world around us and expand our knowledge. It can be found in collective activities and conversation, as well as in the individual moments of reading, looking, listening and reflecting. To study is to apply oneself – to put oneself into play, into action, on the line. There is always a risk involved in study, where we allow ourselves to be possessed by the other[2], and let ourselves be changed by an encounter with the world[3].

The teacher and *the student* are roles that we can step in and out of. When entering a classroom, it usually comes with a contract, where we lend ourselves to these roles.[4] In an educational setting the contract is in the form of a curriculum, where expectations and responsibilities are clearly stated, while in other spaces the terms of study can be less defined. There are also spaces where we come together to study without anyone taking the role of the teacher, in a collective effort to study. In this project I mainly examine the role of the teacher, with the acknowledgement that it is not a role that is fixed, and that differs with the wide range of settings where teaching happens.

1 Audre Lorde, *Sister Outsider* (New York, NY: Random House Inc., 1984), 98. "The learning process is something you can incite, literally incite, like a riot."

2 Stefano Harney and Fred Moten, *The Undercommons: Fugitive Planning & Black Study* (Wivenhoe: Minor Compositions, 2013), 110.

3 Gert Biesta, *The Rediscovery of Teaching* (New York, NY and Oxon: Routledge, 2017).

4 In an exercise I often use, we try to identify the characteristics of the teacher, the student and the artist based on inner and outer expectations, to better our understanding of how these roles play out.

The experimental part of this PhD project has taken the form of guided meditations. This is where I have ventured out into what is unknown territory for me. I chose this format partly because it is the most embarrassing to me – I blush when I tell people of the guided meditations. I take this shame as a sign that there is something to investigate here; something unsafe, something concealed, something unresolved. An experiment is a test constructed to deduct knowledge from a hypothesis or a set of questions. In this case, the assumption is, that to develop pedagogies of the unknown we need to engage all our senses in the service of imagination. This is not a yes or no question, but rather a question of how – how can we identify and develop pedagogies that make use of all our senses? What are the practices of study that can support our engagement in the unknown? The guided meditation is an artistic attempt to form an experimental classroom, a focused place to study, where attention is brought to our embodied relationship to knowledge. The body takes the place as a site of learning and study that has the potential to unsettle and refigure deep seated ideas and habits.

Just like my artistic practice, this experiment plays out in the intersection of performance and pedagogy. The format has travelled between spaces, depending on the invitations that have come my way, and has been adapted accordingly. In an academic setting the guided meditations are presented as a lecture or as an exercise in workshops, while in an art space they take the form of a participatory performance or a sound installation. I have published one guided meditation online as a sound piece for headphones, and I have held workshops in art spaces centred around guided meditations as a creative practice. The construction of the guided meditations is site specific, that is, they are written and performed in relation to the place, the building and its surroundings, as well as to the people and participants.

This dissertation is made in the field of artistic research. The subject and questions are formed from an artistic practice, and presented mainly in a context of contemporary art and the academic art field. Artistic research in the Phd-in-Practice program is practice based, that is, it uses the practice of making art to investigate a subject. The practice is equal to the theoretic reasoning, as they supplement and inform each other. There is often a fluidity between the two, as practising art develops to a form of thinking and the making of theory – theorizing – can be considered a practice. Art relates to knowing and knowledge in unconventional ways, across and beyond academic traditions, which I believe makes artistic research particularly suitable to investigate this subject.

Limitations: I will touch on some discussions from psychology and medicine on the functions of hypnosis and guided meditation, but I will not make any extensive mapping of this field, as this dissertation is not intended for medical research. Neither will there be any overview of all the traditions of guided meditations in different cultures and religions, since my focus is not to make a sociological analysis of the phenomenon but rather to contribute to the field of performance in contemporary art and pedagogy in an art context.[5]

In artistic research, the artistic practice informs how the findings of the research are presented. The art that is produced within a PhD project can be part of both method, experiment and conclusion. This means that you can find the results of my research both in this written reflection and in the actual guided meditations themselves. My aim is to contribute with knowledge, questions and ideas that can be implemented by other artist-teachers and teacher-artists, in other classrooms. I hope you will feel inclined to quote my work not just in academic terms, but in artistic ways as well.

The conditions for making this PhD have been formed by a lack of funding, commuting to another country and the need to support a family at home. This has made the process vulnerable to circumstance, struggling to find the time and resources necessary, dependent on invitations and collaborations, and created an all but straightforward process. Although it has been frustrating, this process has led me to unexpected spaces and audiences, and unforeseen breaks have given me the time to reflect on the work that has

5 Darlings that were cut: playing the double bind in Octavia Butler's parables; deep listening with Pauline Olivero; shape shifting in Swedish and Saami folklore; Donna Haraway's troubled future; the tradition of study circles and utopian thinking in the Swedish labour movement of the 1900s; imagination as negative space.

been done and change directions more than once. The motivation for making a PhD has been to validate my practice and to become better grounded and more adventurous in what I do, both in the classroom and the gallery space. Simultaneously, I wanted to start a conversation on pedagogies in-and-out-of art. I hope this work will lead to more interesting studies, for myself and others. I see this dissertation as a place to start.

I: MAPPING OUR PEDAGOGICAL RELATIONSHIP TO THE UNKNOWN

I invite you to join my search for a radical pedagogy. We will take sight at the horizon and travel across utopia, through the sticky swamps of colonialism, over the fields of hopeful dreams, towards the mountains of promise... But, just as we are about to reach the horizon we will change direction, recalibrate our compass, and steer towards the unknown. Landing with our feet on unfamiliar ground, we will try to find our bearings in the mist of uncertainty.

The search for a radical pedagogy

Pe
Da
Go
Gy

Pedagogy

Pedagogy, pedagogy, pedagogy, pedagogy, pedagogy, pedagogy, pedagogy,
pedagogy, pedagogy, pedagogy, pedagogy, pedagogy, pedagogy, pedagogy,
pedagogy, pedagogy, pedagogy, pedagogy, pedagogy, pedagogy, pedagogy.

Excerpt from *Adrift* – A POETIC POWER POINT, PRESENTATION (2015)

PICK THE WORD INTO PIECES and put it together again. Use your tongue, your cheeks, your lips and your vocal cords to enunciate. Feel your whole face engage with this workout. Break open your voice, speak the word out loud in the room and listen to it reverb back to you. Pe-da-go-gy.

The word pedagogy is present in several languages, but its meaning differs. In some languages and contexts it is used to talk about children and upbringing, in others it addresses education on all levels[6]. In philosophy on teaching, it is often used as an umbrella term for teaching methods, or didactics, and education both formal and informal, as well as for how the transmission of knowledge is structured in all kinds of institutions (the pedagogy of a state, for example). In this text, I use pedagogy in this broader sense of the word. I think of pedagogy as how we structure situations of learning,

6 A pedagogue, in Denmark for example, refers to someone working with children, while in Sweden it refers to anyone working with teaching.

whether it be in a classroom, an auditorium, on Zoom, in an art gallery, in a performance, or in an art installation. Pedagogy includes the act of teaching as well as the act of studying, and how these practices overlap and are intertwined.

A large part of my artistic practice has been dedicated to the search for a radical pedagogy, that is, for the radical possibilities of pedagogy to induce change. I have used pedagogy as a way of bridging my work in teaching, organizing and performance, looking for alternative ways to structure workshops, lectures, performances or other artworks; in different classrooms, self-organized spaces and art institutions.

After finishing my master studies, I found a long time collaborator in Johanna Gustavsson. We initiated Malmö Free University for Women – MFK, a feminist organization for art and knowledge exchange (2006–2011)[7]. MFK started as a community building project, based in our feminist networks in and around Malmö, with an aim to get feminists from activism, art and academia in the same room, to share our knowledge and study together. For five years we arranged hundreds of activities together with our community, first in our own space, and later on in collaboration with different art institutions. We arranged workshops in experimental radio broadcasting, intersectionality, bird watching, queer folk dance, feminist parenting and much more. By the end we published the book *Do the Right Thing – a manual from MFK*[8] with the intent of sending our knowledge forward. From the experience of running a free university we formed a think tank on *radical pedagogy*, where we kept on exploring the possibilities of pedagogy in dialogue with a network of colleagues who work in the intersection of art and pedagogy (2011-2015)[9].

Our pedagogical work was heavily influenced by the work of Bra-

---

7 You can find out more about MFK at http://www.lisanyberg.net/malmo-fria-kvinnouniversitet-mfk-2006-2011/ or at our old website http://mfkuniversitet.blogspot.com/

8 *Do the Right Thing – a manual from MFK* is available for download at http://www.lisanyberg.net/do-the-right-thing-a-manual-from-mfk/

9 Lisa Nyberg and Johanna Gustavsson, "Radikal Pedagogik," accessed March 6, 2017, http://radikalpedagogik.blogspot.com/.

zilian educator and social theorist Paulo Freire. In his understanding of pedagogy, everyone brings knowledge from their lived experience to the classroom, and the role of pedagogy is to create situations where this knowledge can be validated and shared[10]. The aim of our studies were not only to generate knowledge but political subjects; people who was able to act from what they knew, transform their own living situation and in so doing transform society. We wanted to expose power structures by questioning not only *what* we learn but *how* we learn, how we use knowledge and who defines what is worth knowing. Our explicit aim was "to activate a critical thinking and to challenge the prevailing power structures through an active construction of alternatives."[11]

The pedagogies we developed were mainly focused on trying to find alternative ways of teaching and studying together, that could encompass the range of different forms of knowledge, as well as the different people involved with our free university. The ways we had been taught, in school and in the art academy, did not suffice in capturing the scope of knowledge we wanted to bring forth. We were not professional educators, neither were most of the people we invited or who asked to come. Finding ways that enabled anyone to share what they knew, was part of our effort to convince our community that the knowledge they had was worth sharing. Our work was very much practice based – we tried out and developed different formats that would allow anyone to teach, and that lead us to a pedagogical foundation that was radically different from what we knew from school or the academy. Our development of pedagogy was intertwined with the radical effort to strengthen our community's sense that we could institute a shared centre of knowledge – a university.

MFK was defined as a feminist space. We came together primarily as feminists, although with different backgrounds, and the main part of our activities was aimed at anyone who would identify as a

10 Paulo Freire, *Pedagogy of the Oppressed* (London: Penguin Books, 1970); Paulo Freire, *Education for Critical Consciousness* (London. New York.: Continuum, 1974).

11 Nyberg and Gustavsson, "Radikal Pedagogik."

woman[12]. Organizing on the basis of the category "women" made it necessary to elevate all the differences within that category. When we started, the idea of intersectionality was beginning to take root in Scandinavia, and it became a recurring subject. Intersectionality is a perspective where categories that form the basis of oppression, like gender, class, ethnicity, race, sexuality etc. can never be understood in isolation, but in how they are affected and transformed by one another. Therefore, the knowledge we have is partial to our specific position in this matrix, and plural in that it contains elements of all the different social and identity constructs we inherit. We studied the writings of Kimberlé Crenshaw and Patricia Hill Collins, together with writers based in Scandinavia such as Nina Lykke, Kerstin Sandell and Diana Mulinari. We offered workshops where we tried to figure out how to implement these ideas into practice, and make our analysis actionable.

Our idea of what could be considered *radical* was founded in our interpretation of intersectional feminism, and how that could inform the way we organized our teaching, as well as the content of it. It related to whom we invited, how we addressed a subject bearing in mind different power positions and how we exposed conflicting interests within a group defined by gender. Intersectionality helped us think about how we defined our space, how we could create a space of difference, with room for conflict, but also to build unholy alliances. It made us speak about our privileges, not only our oppression. The writings of Audre Lorde and Chandra Mohanty helped us recognize difference as a strength and interdependence as a necessity for change. We tried to be transparent in terms of hierarchies and power positions, and allow for the complexity of intersecting identity formations to exist, in efforts that were often both uncomfortable and sparked conflict. Getting people in a room together was more important than harmony or resolve.[13]

---

12 Our definition was "everyone who, now or at some point, identify as women", including trans and non-binary folks, and we were careful never to impose identification on other people.

13 Read more about our work in the publication *Do the Right Thing – a manual from MFK*, available at http://www.lisanyberg.net/do-the-right-thing-a-manual-from-mfk/

Derived from the Latin *radix*, meaning root, *radical* admits that change is possible, and that change demands that we go to the roots of the matter. Radical change runs deeper than the surface of things. It digs down to what lies beneath, to unearth the systems that support and nourish what blossoms and ripens before our eyes. Radical implies a change that is groundbreaking, a systemic shift from where there is no re-settling into old ways. It is a risky practice, as it is challenging the status quo.

Radical pedagogies aim to change the value systems of knowledge, and the structures of learning and education in a fundamental way, from the ground up. We find in this category all the pedagogies that stem from social movements; decolonial, feminist, anti-fascist, queer pedagogies, and many others. They differ from the field of critical pedagogy in that they do not only focus on the established institutions for education, but recognize that teaching and learning happen in many places; in the classroom, in the schoolyard, in the university, at home, at the workplace, in sports, in state politics, in families, in political movements, in art. A radical pedagogy searches for pedagogy's radical possibilities, inside and outside education. It strives towards an epistemological shift – a shift in what we consider knowledge or worth knowing; how we learn to learn, including our desires for knowing, what knowledge we long for. Pedagogy is one of the roots that needs to be re-examined within a bigger project of systemic change.

Radical, in itself, does not give direction for this change. There are radical socialists and radical feminists as well as radical fascists and radical nationalists. This means that we need to be adamant in how we position ourselves. For me, this means a position on the side of justice and liberation for the oppressed, marginalized and dispossessed, advocating for thorough political or social change. The possibility for change that the space of the unknown opens up, needs to be entered with the intent of a more just and free world.

The company I keep uses radical as a quality/attribute of pedagogy: for bell hooks it is about transgressing, for M. Jacqui Alexander it is about being uncompromised, for Gayatri Chakravorty Spivak it is about the epistemological shift. Radical can always stand at the risk of being an empty placeholder for something "rad" as in edgy, risky and brave. Rather, I would claim that radical is the insistence that we aim for the roots of things, that we are willing to look at those deep-set structures and challenge them. It entails the notion that one is willing to do the fundamental, dirty work of digging at the roots, or looking up the stream; both far-reaching and thorough. Our use of *radical* must be defined and continuously redefined. As I will try to show you in this dissertation, it does not come with a set goal, or a series of methods or schemes. My search for a radical pedagogy is ongoing.

The intersectional feminist grounding of my work, is tied to the epistemological insight that knowledge is both partial and plural. Partial entails that we all have a partial view of the world, framed by our identities, histories, experiences and our position in society. We see things from where we stand and our position taints our interpretation of the world. We see things in proximity to ourselves, and we choose which directions to set our gaze. Our outlook makes us blind to what is not within our scope.

This means that every knowledge is also an ignorance. Vanessa de Oliveira Andreotti, indigenous scholar and professor in educational studies, confronts the idea of progression in traditional education. Instead of a dramaturgy of education that turns ignorance into knowledge, she suggests another relation between the two (inspired by Spivak's work on "the righting of wrongs"). She writes:

> "Perhaps a starting point is a shift in the understanding of knowledge from 'knowledge versus ignorance' toward 'every knowledge is also an ignorance' (of other knowledges). The body of literature I draw on affirms that *'wrongs' are caused by knowledge too*. The 'every knowledge is an ignorance' approach requires an understanding of how knowledges are produced, how they relate to power and how they may shape subjectivities and relationships in conscious and non-conscious ways."[14]

14 Vanessa de Oliveira (Andreotti), "Education, Knowledge and the Righting of Wrongs," *Other Education: The Journal of Educational Alternatives* 1, no. 1 (2012): 23.

THIS UNSETTLES THE IDEA of the teacher lifting the student out of ignorance, and puts students and teachers in a position of being equally knowing and equally ignorant, although in different and shifting ways. It adds another layer to Paulo Freire's notion that everyone has and brings knowledge; that this is not only an additive process, but a contradictory one loaded with possible conflict; my knowledge might confront and question your knowledge; your knowledge might come from an erasure of mine; I might not be able to tell you what I know in a language that you can understand.

At times, it can be necessary to keep some knowledges partial. There are narratives only some people know, that are inaccessible to others, that have had to be shielded from being appropriated and conformed to fit hegemonic science structures. In decolonial theory there is value assigned to protecting some knowledges; narratives that are not made accessible to everyone, and that is how things need to be, at least for the time being. Some knowledges need to be strategically kept within a community, in light of the ongoing consequences of the destruction of indigenous history and language made by colonization[15].

Plurality means that there is not one singular, universal truth about the world. No one person has the full picture. This challenges the hierarchical structure of knowledge that traditional education largely depends on. When we come together it is in a plurality of voices, a choir of different tones. This plurality is not something that needs to be consolidated; there is strength in difference[16]. Different voices make for a complex sound, that may contain harmonies as well as contradictions. Together we can make better sense of what is happening to us. We depend on each other to create a fuller view of the world. Plurality can also be situated in one person's voice, making her sound contradictory, irrational and as if she does not "make sense". The intersection of multiple cultures and identity formations in one person can result in a plural voice, that might not be understood within the frames of hegemonic epistemology[17].

---

15 Jane Anderson, "Negotiating Who 'Owns' Penobscot Culture," *Anthropological Quarterly* 91, no. 1 (2018): 267–305.

16 Lorde, *Sister Outsider*.

17 Trinh T Minh-ha, *Woman, Native, Other. Writing Postcoloniality and Feminism*. (Bloomington and Indianapolis: Indiana University Press, 1989).

For this project, it is especially interesting how a feminist epistemology of partial and plural knowledge exposes how *not knowing is built into our ways of knowing*. The unknown is in a mutual relationship with the known. The unknown is not apart from us, at a distance as an unknown territory to be explored, but the unknown is an intrinsic aspect of life and learning. It is at the heart of our lives. Hence, education does not need to claim a universal truth about the world to aspire to, and is not dependent on progression from ignorant to knowing to assert its pedagogy. Understanding the world does not need to be stipulated as an end goal, but rather as an ongoing process and action. Studying becomes an endless adventure, a *scuola senza fine*[18], a school without an end.

Thinking about knowledge as partial and plural, means that the unknown cannot be eradicated, but have to be dealt and worked with. Allowing for this complexity to inform our studies is hard work, both frustrating and painful at times. To comprehend and hold space for partiality and plurality is almost impossible for one person to do alone – it requires a collective. Speaking from a place of uncertainty demands a level of trust that is not easily obtained. In many classrooms this community of trust is not in place. Sometimes we speak out anyway, on behalf of complexity, but it is an exhausting practice and we will have to take turns. Simultaneously, we will have to work to create those kinds of classrooms where holding complexity and uncertainty is possible. Spaces where learning becomes much more occupied with listening to others, being in conversation with others, "thinking together as work to be done"[19].

Unsettling utopia as a pedagogical frame

With MFK we made a series of investigations into the future unknown, through workshops and lock-ins [20]. Imagining a feminist utopia became an important exercise for us to be able to think about and

---

18 Adriana Monti, *Scuola Senza Fine*, 1983, http://www.universitadelledonne.it/english/scuola%20senza%20fine.htm. A film about the 150 hours reform in Italy that we did a screening of at MFK.

19 Isabelle Stengers, *In Catastrophic Times: Resisting the Coming Barbarism* (Lüneburg: Open Humanities Press, meson press, 2015), 132.

20 The "lock-ins" were 48 hour intense workshops where we locked ourselves in without phones or any outside stimuli, to imagine a different world outside.

relate to the future. Utopia came to us in the form of a question from a friend: *What happens when we win?* We rejected this question at first (Who has time for such thinking? We have urgent work to do!) but it made us look up from the grind of our day-to-day organizing and activist work, to look to where we were heading: towards the horizon.

We made a series of workshops that address utopia performatively, by enacting the future we wanted in a series of collective imaginations.[21] We gave ourselves permission to temporarily free ourselves from the politics of the here and now, and to re-think current iterations of the state, nation, family, religion and so forth. The workshops provided us with valuable perspectives on how our work was fitted within a movement, that stretched in time from past – present – future, and prompted us to examine our desires, longings and expectations. The workshops were often intense, emotional experiences, accommodating both sadness, anger and joy when being confronted with other possibilities to organize life that had not yet been realized.

The more we worked with utopia, the more we came to understand it as an empowering and community building method. It provided a space for us to come together and collectively imagine different feminist futures. Coming together, not only as response to acute oppressive politics, but as a creative collective with visions on how to construct a society, turned out to be of real value to us: it supported our need to visualize what we wanted to work towards, and prompted us to define what questions really mattered to us and enabled us to set a political agenda on our own terms. It provided a temporary escape to a place where we had the time and space to be together, where negotiation started from a place of mutual trust and recognition, away from political games and power plays. It gave us new energy and an expanded view on our work.

---

21 "Malmö Free University for Women (MFK) hereby cordially invites you to take part in a collective staging of a feminist utopia! Let's treat ourselves to a temporary amnesia about the practical aspects of the here and now and try to visualize an INTENSE ECSTATIC FUTURE together." The workshops took place at 16 Beaver Group in New York, Konsthall C in Stockholm, at art academies and more. A step-by-step instruction in Johanna Gustavsson and Lisa Nyberg, *Do the Right Thing*, 2011, available at http://www.lisanyberg.net/do-the-right-thing-a-manual-from-mfk/

But, for dealing with the future as an unknown, as change, utopia as method had its limitations. Even though we freed ourselves from set formats such as-isms (temporarily banning words like capitalism, socialism, fascism and so on) and allowed ourselves to imagine utopias in different space-times (for instance; utopia could be set up for an island, for the whole Earth, or for a solar system) and utopias that were constantly changing (shifting with every new generation, or bound in a constant pendulum between revolution and contra-revolution), there was a limit to how much unpredictability could be built into our visions. We had a tendency to keep control over future generations, as well as over Earth's resources; we were giving too much power to ourselves and failing to acknowledge a world that keeps on changing.

We were confronted with a resistance, in ourselves as well as in others, to examine the unresolvable contradictions and costs of utopia; to decide who would be included and excluded and to define at what and whose expense a process would be implemented. It proved difficult to confront or ignore existing conflicts, like land rights, without falling back into old, useless patterns. There was a tendency to wanting the world to be presented as a clean slate, clearing away all the rubble of history, before any progress could be made. We were frustrated by our incapability to productively draw the link from that future place to the historically situated struggles of women, queer, working class, POC, Black and indigenous folks. The hopefulness we felt in that room where we staged our utopia, seemed to slip away as soon as we exited the space.

In the end, the utopia workshops left us frustrated. Our attempts to imagine otherwise could not capture the sense of uncertainty and unpredictability that is a fundamental aspect of the present, and of any situation of oppression. We came to the conclusion that utopia, as a pedagogical effort to engage with the future, though it had offered us a lot, was not enough.

There are many ways to make the future present. We do it inadvertently through our expectations, dreams, hopes and imaginations, and more consciously when we set up possible scenarios that we plan for. We engage with the future by picturing how things will go, and how they could be. Imagining things differently – imagining otherwise – and specifically imagining towards the future, has in a Western literary canon been dominated by ideas of utopia. Since the novel *Utopia* by Thomas More in 1516, the idea of "the good place which is no place" has been the go-to of future imagining, and is as such worthy of critical investigation[22]. What is the role of utopia in studying for a future unknown?

More's novel is a story of a land inhabited by natives, that is being colonized by the Utopians. The Utopians establish a nation by digging a canal that cuts off the nation from the mainland, and proceed by establishing a culture that fulfills their idealized dreams of efficient development and prosperity. The natives are assimilated to the culture of the settlers, and those who do not want to assimilate are rejected and displaced. The story is told from the perspective of the settler. From their point of view, it is a story of success – the land is considered empty until it is properly civilized, and this civilization is to the benefit of all[23].

Lorenzo Veracini, an associate professor at Swinburne's Institute for Social Research in Australia, has named this process "settler indigenisation"[24]. In this process, the settler and the native switch places, making the settler indigenous to the land by claiming the role as natural inhabitants of the land, while the indigenous peoples are, in Veracini's words, "de-naturalized"[25]. Veracini has done the work of distinguishing between colonization and settler colonization, where within colonization, the colonizer expanded from their territory in search of natural resources with the aim to later return to the homeland, whereas within settler colonialism, the settler has come to stay, and in staying continue to erase the indigenous peoples and their culture.[26]

Utopia, in the tradition developed from More's novel, has functioned as a theory of civilization. Karl Hardy, professor in Cultural

---

22 Stephen Duncombe, *Thomas More Open Utopia* (Minor Compositions, 2012).

23 Duncombe.

24 Lorenzo Veracini, *The Settler Colonial Present* (Springer, 2015), 38.

25 Veracini, 38.

26 Lorenzo Veracini, "Introducing Settler Colonial Studies," *Settler Colonial Studies* 1, no. 1 (2011): 1–12.

Studies at Queen's University, engages with the emergent critical discourses on settler colonization to "unsettle hope" and demands that the field of utopian studies looks critically at its foundation. According to Hardy, progressive modernity relied on distancing itself from the primitive through the faculty of reason, that legitimated sovereignty over land and natives, through displacement, assimilation or war.[27]

To dispute the claim to universality made by some utopian scholars, Hardy argues that the idea of non-place is not utopian for indigenous peoples. The right to land is an essential political conflict for most indigenous peoples, and the particularity of place is a fundamental epistemological and ontological referent. Place in many ways defines indigeneity.[28] There is social dreaming in indigenous communities as well, but it does not align with a colonial, utopian construction. Western forms of utopia are not broad enough to encompass all the social dreaming and are not useful for all hopeful practices.

Creating utopia as a universal longing ignores the ways that future imaginings are imbued by the present. It suggests the future as empty space, as "neutral" space, or as unused land: a blank slate that can be filled with the hopeful fantasies of the present. It evades being accountable for the historical acts that have led up to this moment, as well as the different iterations of history that was not written by its beneficiaries. A universalist utopia stands at risk of erasing all the different presents that exist simultaneously, and the possible futures that could come from them. It also ignores other ways to relate to the future that are not linear in the Western sense of a timeline.

There have been attempts to re-articulate utopia, away from claims to universality. Ernst Bloch, a German Marxist philosopher born in 1885, has written extensively on utopia, and his writing has been picked up during the last couple of decades by contemporary utopian scholars, such as José Muñoz and Ruth Levitas. Bloch found

27 Karl Hardy, "Unsettling Hope: Contemporary Indigenous Politics, Settler-Colonialism, and Utopianism," *Spaces of Utopia: An Electronic Journal* 2, no. 1 (2012): 123–36.

28 Hardy, 124.

a form of anticipatory consciousness in the notion of the *not-yet*. The not-yet makes a bridge between the present and the future, in the duality of its notion; the *not* – a current lack, something missing – and the *yet* – what is to come, an anticipated future. In the individual this bridge resides as the *not-yet-conscious*, a utopian impulse that takes a creative outlet, on the brink of becoming conscious. It can be detected in the art we make and the stories we tell. Simultaneously the not-yet is the collective strive of a society, a world of becoming, a horizon of future possibilities.[29] To Bloch, this anticipatory consciousness is an unavoidable and indispensable element in the production of the future.[30]

Ruth Levitas, a British professor of Sociology, draws on Bloch when she defines utopia as a method. As such, she explores utopian aspects of culture as they are expressed through everyday acts by individuals and collectives: "Utopia, [in the sense of Bloch's not-yet] does not require the imaginative construction of whole other worlds. It occurs as an embedded element in a vast range of human practice and culture."[31] These are practices beyond the imagination of an ideal state, like longing, wishing, planning and predicting. Levitas finds that utopia does not only contain hopeful practices that project towards the future, but also refusal – a refusal to accept that there is no alternative – and as such impacts our experience of the present.

Levitas recognizes the aspect of failure in utopia as well, advocating for failure as a necessary component of utopia as method. She finds in Bloch the proclamation that hope carries disappointment; that utopian feelings can, and often will be, disappointed. "The recognition of necessary failure leads to the insistence on the provisionality of utopia. It is a method of considering the future, not the stipulation of a goal."[32] The expected disappointment or failure of utopia, safeguards social dreaming from falling into totalitarianism.

---

29 Ernst Bloch, *The Principle of Hope Volume I* (Cambridge, Massachusetts: MIT Press, 1953), 6.

30 Ruth Levitas, "Looking for the Blue: The Necessity of Utopia," *Journal of Political Ideologies* 12:3 (2007): 291.

31 Levitas, 291.

32 Levitas, 303.

Bloch and Levitas offer us a chance to consider the future as something radically different than the present, without stipulating exactly how that future will take form, and with the acknowledgment that our expectations will disappoint. They help us engage with the future, without certainty. Utopia as method is more analytic than descriptive. It looks to the ways we experience the not-yet in our everyday, and the hopeful practices we lean on. It recognizes how these practices function as acts of refusal to accept a narrative that stipulates that there are no alternatives to our present condition.

What is the role of hope in imagining otherwise? What are the possibilities of hope in the face of hopelessness? Jem Bendell, a British professor of Sustainability Leadership, took a few months off in 2018 to get updated on the latest data from climate scientists. In his paper "Deep Adaptation: A Map for Navigating Climate Tragedy" he summarises his findings, sharing a reality that turned out to be much worse than what he could have ever imagined. It forced him to accept that we are facing "inevitable collapse, probable catastrophe and possible extinction."[33] In the process of accepting this new reality, he had to abandon the hope that he had previously clung to; the hope that corporate sustainability and an innovation would be enough to turn this development around. He found himself in a state of despair.

Insisting on looking for hope in the face of hopelessness, Bendell found that there is something more beyond despair. Despair is not constant; it is a state that can be moved through. As an example, a death sentence does not necessarily make people give up on their lives. Rather, many seem to re-examine their life choices, and make changes to accommodate those new priorities. They find a way to accept the facts of their situation and to uncover a new direction. Beyond despair there is another form of hope. When we give up our hold on this world, when we abandon our hopes for this way of life, it opens the capacity to imagine other, previously unimaginable

33 Jem Bendell, "Deep Adaptation: A Map for Navigating Climate Tragedy," *IFLAS Occasional Paper* 2, July 2018, http://lifeworth.com/deepadaptation.pdf.

futures. Bendell found that in the midst of pain and grief, he started to define and tend to the most important things in life, and to have the really hard and deep conversations with his friends and community.[34]

Some people would suggest we should not talk about the consequences of climate change, as it may render people fearful, hopeless and passive. That our anxiety will overtake us, and we will surrender to our faith and give up. Bendell's journey lead him to develop a pedagogical framework that could hold conversations based in the reality of climate change. It is centred around three qualities for deep adaptation, taking the form of three questions: "Resilience asks us 'how do we keep what we really want to keep?' Relinquishment asks us 'what do we need to let go of in order to not make matters worse?' Restoration asks us 'what can we bring back to help us with the coming difficulties and tragedies?'"[35] These questions have supported Bendell in having conversations and workshops, with young people and adults, that do not end in despair, but open up our imagination to confront catastrophe, to think about what life could be within and after catastrophe.

Ernst Bloch makes a distinction that differentiates between politically passive and active forms of hope. He takes hope out of the escapist realm of what he calls "compensatory hope", a hopefulness that compensates for the burdens of the everyday through for instance daydreaming, to his notion of "educated hope". The premise for Bloch is that hope is something that can be learned. Educated hope is not a simple escape from our troubles, but builds on the knowledge from the social struggles of our history. To Bloch, working in a Marxist tradition, hope is decidedly material and possible by will and action. Educated hope is willful: "The work of this emotion requires people to throw themselves actively into what is becoming, to which they themselves belong."[36]

---

34 Amisha Ghadiali, "E45 – Jem Bendell on Deep Adaptation, Climate Change and Societal Collapse // Acceptance and Evolution in the Face of Global Meltdown," accessed May 19, 2020, https://www.thefutureisbeautiful.co/2018/12/27/e45-jem-bendell-on-deep-adaptation-climate-change-and-societal-collapse-acceptance-and-evolution-in-the-face-of-global-meltdown/.

35 Bendell, "Deep Adaptation: A Map for Navigating Climate Tragedy," 23.

36 Bloch, *The Principle of Hope Volume I*, 4.

Educated hope could mean just this; to face the reality of what our world is going through and still insist that we belong in this future, and will have to find ways to throw ourselves actively into it. It gives us the opportunity to engage with the future, without succumbing to banal optimism or political evasiveness. This hope is based on the recognition that political struggles have changed the course of history and will continue to do so. Educated hope suggests that hope is something we can learn, which means that pedagogy has a role to play in *how* we hope for the future, in face of the unknown.

A pedagogy based on educated hope could look like the deep adaptation framework that Bendell suggests: finding openings that help us move through despair. Questions we can ask ourselves and each other that we can hold on to in a painful process of letting go, that support us in our grief, and calm us in our fear. Questions that will help us find our bearings.

In the guided meditations that I am proposing, the openings take the form of suggestions; proposals for thinking, imagining and making connections to the unknown. I am trying to strike the balance for educated hope; not being naïvely hopeful or merely compensating for uncomfortable feelings, while not prescribing how hope should play out. Instead, insisting that our acts in the present matter for the future, and that hope can be located in the unknown. As American writer Rebecca Solnit suggests:

> "Hope locates itself in the premises that we don't know what will happen and that in the spaciousness of uncertainty is room to act. When you recognise uncertainty, you recognise that you may be able to influence the outcomes – you alone or you in concert with a few dozen or several million others. Hope is an embrace of the unknown and the unknowable, an alternative to the certainty of both optimists and pessimists. Optimists think it will all be fine without our involvement; pessimists adopt the opposite position; both excuse themselves from acting. It is the belief that what we do matters even though how and when it may matter, who and what it

> may impact, are not things we can know beforehand. We may not, in fact, know them afterwards either, but they matter all the same, and history is full of people whose influence was most powerful after they were gone."[37]

HOPE MIGHT NOT ALWAYS LOOK LIKE we would expect it to. It takes hard work to let go of hope, only to try to find it again, in a different form: letting go of hope for things to stay the same, trying to find hope for something other, for changes. Educated hope stresses the import ance of considering a future, even when it will fail us. In sight of the urgency of climate change and fascist political tendencies, not giving up is crucial. And for that, some form of hope is necessary.

With MFK, our work with utopia prompted in us a question of how to deal with the unknown when imagining otherwise. How could we approach the future without trying to predict it, as something unknowable, and rest in the uncertainty of not knowing without losing the will to work for political change? Listening to Bloch and Levitas, maybe we could have better accepted our failures and dealt with the possibility of disappointment. We could have studied towards a more educated hope, and valued our anticipation for the future as something that could strengthen our movement, and maybe protect us from pessimistic politics.

Despite its limitation, utopia took us out of one place and into something other. It changed our perspective, even though we did not really figure out what to do next. Utopia as method does not necessarily need to be discarded, as long as it is one of many hopeful practices, to be used carefully, and supplemented with other methodologies and storytelling practices. Practices that do not hold on to an idyllic ending, but still offer places where to start.

37 Rebecca Solnit, *Hope in the Dark: Untold Histories Wild Possibilities* (Edinburgh: Canongate Books, 2016). xii

Imagining otherwise

How do we relate to the unknown through our imagination? How do we activate those openings, that spaciousness, that the unknown opens for us? How do we fill this space with dreams and imaginations? Imagining otherwise in not only about telling alternative stories – it is about *how* we imagine, our practices of imagining, and how to train for imagination. Imagining is not effortless. As adults, for the most part, imagination does not hold a definite space in our lives. Despite the emphasis on creativity as a motor in our society, in terms of innovation and development, the boundaries within which we are encouraged to imagine are still very limited. Imagination is seldom valued beyond what it can do to support economic growth.

The skills to imagine freely are not easily obtained. If we value imagination and creativity as something more than an economic booster; as an important skill for its potential to transgress hegemonic boundaries – how do we train the mind to imagine beyond what we already know? How do we learn to develop practices of imagining that factor our interconnectedness with others; with other people and beings, with our bodies, with ghosts and ancestors, with our history and our future? How do we learn to imagine in a way that changes the now?

I turn to post-colonial intellectual and feminist scholar Gayatri Chakravorty Spivak to frame the case for an aesthetic education. Spivak's theoretical work has always been in conversation with her teaching and, as a teacher of teachers in rural India and a professor in Comparative Literature at Columbia University, epistemology has a prominent place in her work. Her experience of teaching literature is at the center of her reasoning on the subject of aesthetic education, and a major part of her writing on the subject from the 1990s and onward can be found in the book *An Aesthetic Education in the Era of Globalization* (2012).

Spivak's trust in aesthetic education is based on the premise that it is a place for training the imagination and teaching the subject how to play. Spivak's project for an education that imagines otherwise, is about an epistemological shift; the need for an epistemic change in the face of the post-colonial imperialism that is globalization. An epistemological shift can be said to be a shift in what we consider knowledge or worth knowing; how we learn to learn, including our desires for knowing, what knowledges we long for. The condition of the present is dominated by an epistemic violence, an othering of the so called "third world" towards the West. The aim, according to Spivak, for an aesthetic education is "an un-coercive re-arrangement of desires", that is; to re-arrange desires away from capitalist and imperialist longings, to other, more ethical objects.

> "I would like to propose that the training of the imagination that can teach the subject to play – an aesthetic education – can also teach it to discover (theoretically or practically) the premises of the habit that obliges us to transcendentalize religion and nation (as Bateson and Freud both point out). If, however, this is only a "rearrangement of desire" or the substitution of one habit for another through pedagogical sleight-of-hand, there will be no ability to recover that discovery for a continuity of epistemological effort. We must learn to do violence to the epistemo-epistemological difference and remember that this is what education 'is' and thus keep up the work of displacing belief onto the terrain of the imagination, attempt to access the epistemic. The displacement of belief onto the terrain of the imagination can be a description of reading in its most robust sense. It is also the irreducible element of an aesthetic education."[38]

By exemplifying with her own teaching in English literature, and the basic act of reading, Spivak introduces the sentiment "displacing belief onto the terrain of imagination" as an irreducible element of all aesthetic education. *Displacement* is a strategical act that Spivak employs to make use of the knowledge from her own European

38 Gayatri Chakravorty Spivak, *An Aesthetic Education in the Era of Globalization* (Cambridge, Massachusetts: Harvard University Press, 2012), 10.

education (with thinkers like Kant, Schiller and DeMan) by shifting the place of a concept or a sentiment, and, as I read it, simultaneously lose control over it. It is an intentional mistake[39]. It is a freeing act. Displacing belief onto the terrain of imagination can be seen as an attempt to restate imagination as fundamental in how we think about and organize society.

Spivak continuously stresses that we cannot solve or rid ourselves of our history or our complicity in how history impacts the present. We are always complicit in the systems and institutions that hold oppressive structures in place. Since we cannot escape these structures, we must learn instead how to play, and we must do it here, in the place where we are right now. Though it might seem impossible to play in the midst of resistance, the call to play offers openings, options and movement when we think that we are stuck.

Spivak claims that aesthetic education trains our imagination and teaches us to play. Art schools offer access to different practices like writing, drawing, painting, singing and dancing etc., as well as encounters with art, in the experience of reading, seeing and sensing art. These are all practices that, in different ways, exercise our imagination. Displacing belief to the terrain of imagination gives us room enough to play, within/on/under/over the restrictions that binds us, without escaping our ignoring our complicity.

Spivak's approach to playing is to use the materials we have at our hands, to make use of all that is available, and she does not let us discard of anything. Instead she asks us to *productively undo* the material we have access to. To unravel, loosen and release what we have before us, so we can find another use for it. To Spivak, productive undoing is done "at the faultlines of the doing, without accusation, without excuse, with a view to use"[40]. Spivak offers us possibilities to mend, reinvent, displace and ab-use as the playful tools that keep us in this balancing act.

Spivak writes this with the Humanities in mind, and how to deal with the ideas and concepts from the Enlightenment, but I think her

39 Spivak, 25.
40 Spivak, 1.

thoughts are transferable to a visual arts education as well. To use what we have inherited from art history – the aesthetic traditions, the craft traditions, the pedagogical traditions as well as traditions of ideas – and productively undo them, for our own use.

To think what is absent or unseen, we use our imagination. Imagination, can be defined as the faculty (the capacity, the power) to make representations appear, with or without an external incentive. Imagination, in the singular human being, is a creative force of the mind, connected to image, form and creation. I take this definition from Cornelius Castoriadis, a Greek-French philosopher, economist and psychologist active in France from the late 1940s and onwards. He found imagination to be a powerful force in individual agency as well as towards collective revolution and autonomy.[41]

Castoriadis identifies the radical potential of imagination. In Aristotle, he detects two different meanings of the term *phantasia* (fantasy, imagination). The first one imitates, reproduces and combines; creating new constellations of what already is. The second meaning of *phantasia* is much more radical, as it possibly pre-seeds every thought, before we even start to define what is real and what is fictitious. Castoriadis calls this *primary imagination*, and it corresponds to what he then proceeds to name *radical imagination*.[42]

Radical imagination creates *ex nihilo*, from nothing (not in nothing, *in nihilo* or with nothing, *cum nihilo*). With this statement, he does not claim that imagination happens in a vacuum, but he makes the distinction that imagination, apart from rearranging what we know into new formations, also have the radical power to form new things, seemingly out of nothing. It exists before language, taking shape without being dependent on words, before our analytical mind kicks in.[43]

Imagination does not only take place in the individual, but has a

41 Disillusioned with the deterministic strands of the Trotskyist Marxism, Castoriadis searched for other ways to understand the process of instituting a new society, and found his inspiration in Aristoteles and Kant, as well as in psychoanalysis.

42 Cornelius Castoriadis, *The Castoriadis Reader / Cornelius Castoriadis. Translated and Edited by David Ames Curtis.* (Oxford, UK. Malden, USA.: Blackwell Publishers Ltd, 1997), 320.

43 Castoriadis, 321.

strong social aspect. We tend to use our imagination in the search for shared meanings. The collective aspects of imagining are often referred to as *the social imaginary*, or simply *the imaginary*. According to Castoriadis the social imaginary is what institutes society. The motivation for the socialization process is the search for shared meaning. In the socialization process the psyche partly abandons its own subjective, self-contained meaning, for the shared meanings provided by society. According to Castoriadis, society is *nothing but* the institution of meanings – by the means of social imaginary significations. The significations we collectively imagine take the form of institutions like religion, norms, family forms, law etc., and as language.[44]

Castoriadis' view of society is that it is always driven by the imaginative force of its members, the desire of people, and it is constantly structuring and instituting into new forms. "Society is creation, and creation of itself: self-creation."[45] This process, of continuously self-instituting and self-altering, is usually very slow, spanning over generations. The condition for society to be truly autonomous (which is the main goal of Castoriadis' revolution), is that it is self-aware of its self-instituting process. It must be able to look at itself and beyond itself. It must be able to question what is.

The double bind of the strong social aspects of imagination, is that it also has a tendency to limit our capacity to imagine. Vanessa de Oliveira Andreotti has pointed to this epistemic blindness – the inability to see beyond a very limited version of reality. Education in its traditional form enforces an entrenched mono-cultural conception of knowledge. European thought tradition has enforced an epistemic domination on large parts of the world. We are taught the right way to think, and to dream, in a way that fits with the house that modernity built. It affects our imagination, and inhibits our ability to imagine beyond the dominant representations, tropes and symbols. According to Andreotti, it is a form of over-socialization of the mind. As an example, she asks us to imagine a corn cob, then

44 Castoriadis, 330.
45 Castoriadis, 332.

juxtaposes that internal image with a photograph of corn cobs in a variety of forms, patterns and colours. Our imagination has been colonized by one variety of corn cob – the yellow one.[46]

Our consciousness needs a break from the world to be able to imagine. Consciousness is knowing *about* something. By acknowledging what we encounter, by being conscious of what is, our consciousness affirms the world. But for consciousness to imagine, it has to distance itself from the world in order to make space for imagination. This gap is where the mind goes beyond. A consciousness that is too tied up with the world as it is, have no space to be creative, or to imagine the unseen or the unthinkable.

Art schools are often described by students as a sacred space, an oasis, a refuge. A place that is somewhat sheltered from the pressures of main society. A place to experiment without the demands of productivity and utility. This is a pedagogical tradition in arts education, I would claim, to support students in their will to transgress. There is teaching going on that supports students in imagining otherwise; classrooms that allow for experimentation, for breaking rules and expectations, for defiance and contradictory interpretations of assignments. Simultaneously, every art academy holds its own hidden curriculum; of forgotten rooms, cellars and attics, unattended workshops, meetings outside the schedule, where things happen beyond the school's control. This is probably true of every school, but maybe more possible in an art school with 24 hour access and a lot of unused space and accessible material.

Imagination is conditioned by this shift in attention. Allowing ourselves to let go of the world for a moment, to dive into the creative flow of our work, to focus our attention on the smallest detail, the slightest shift, and allow for all the unreasonable reasons to make art happen, for the feeling, the intuition, the unspoken stream we feel begged to follow. A place where we can move through the pain, or the joy, or the grief; to transgress. Queer Chicana poet, writer, and feminist theorist Gloria Anzaldúa writes:

46 de Oliveira (Andreotti), "Education, Knowledge and the Righting of Wrongs."

> "To facilitate the 'movies' with soundtracks, I need to be alone, or in a sensory-deprived state. I plug up my ears with wax, put on my black cloth eye-shades, lie horizontal and unmoving, in a state between sleeping and waking, mind and body locked into my fantasy. I am held prisoner by it. My body is experiencing events. In the beginning it is like being in a movie theater, as pure spectator. Gradually I become so engrossed with the activities, the conversations, that I become a participant in the drama. I have to struggle to 'disengage' or escape from my 'animated story,' I have to get some sleep so I can write tomorrow. Yet I am gripped by a story which won't let me go. Outside the frame, I am film director, screenwriter, camera operator. Inside the frame, I am the actors – male and female – I am desert sand, mountain, I am dog, mosquito. I can sustain a four- to six-hour 'movie.' Once I am up, I can sustain several 'shorts' of anywhere between five and thirty minutes. Usually these 'narratives' are the offspring of stories acted out in my head during periods of sensory deprivation."[47]

GLORIA ANZALDÚA offers us an insight into the consequences of taking seriously the connection between body, imagination and creation. She describes the long induction period, working against the resistance, leading herself closer to the painful work of writing. The writing itself is pulling of the flesh, a blood offering. These are no small sacrifices. In the process she deprives herself of senses to be able to imagine, to stay with her body, to place herself in that adaptive state. Lying on her bed she practices to change her thought patterns, re-programming her consciousness. She looks her demons in the face, feeds thoes she wants to grow, and purposefully neglects and starves thoes she wants to leave. While writing other myths, to be and become with.

---

47 Gloria Anzaldúa, *Borderlands/La Frontera: The New Mestiza*, 4th edition (San Francisco, CA: Aunt Lute Books, 1987), 92.

Closing our eyes to meditate can be a fast track to shifting our attention from the visual to attend to other bodily sensations, to our inner life and to our imagination. It gets us "out of our heads" so to speak. So much of our culture depends on the visual. Closing our eyes, when so many of us are accustomed to relying on our eye sight to navigate, can be an act of refusal as well as an act of trust. It makes us vulnerable.[48] Western culture is most concerned with visual clues. The visual is the sense most tied up with reason, seeing is still a measure of truth – to see things clearly. When we prioritize the input from our eyes, we can look without really acknowledging that we have a body. We have trained our minds to disassociate our other sensations from that of looking.

When we close our eyes to the horizon, we tend to imagine the future in a different way. Instead of visualizing the road ahead and trying to predict what is coming, what awaits at the horizon, we tend to the hard work of being present. Being present is an attentive space, a space of listening, sensing, smelling, feeling.[49] From this place, the path to the future might not be so straight.

What might be lost in Spivak's focus on the epistemological, is the significance of the sensory and the ontological. With the conflation of the study of literature with all aesthetic education, something gets lost. The emphasis on literature and written language, sometimes makes her theory seem disembodied. Maybe because of the emphasis on words, and because literature studies is placed within a humanist tradition, which visual arts and performing arts education are not. I miss a reflection on how knowledge is not only in our heads, but we know in our bodies, learn through our senses, and imagine with them too.[50] As Vietnamese filmmaker, writer and post-colonial theorist Trinh T. Minh-ha writes: "But thought is as

48 A reminder: this vulnerability is lived everyday by people on the spectrum of sight limitation and blindness. To learn more, look to Disability studies and Crip theory.

49 Through mediation we can access a trance state, what in hypnotherapy is also called an adaptive state. More on this subject can be found in Chapter II.

50 Walter S Gershon, "Double Binds, Ab-Uses, and a Hopeless Hope: Epistemological Possibilities and Sensual Questions for Spivak's Introductory Framing of An Aesthetic Education in the Era of Globalization," *Critical Literacy: Theories and Practices* 9, no. 1 (2015).

much a product of the eye, the finger, or the foot as it is of the brain."[51]

> *Listen to your body, listen for a rhythm. Your body, as any body with a pulse, is never really still. There is always movement; small shifts of weight from one side to the other, muscles tensing up or relaxing, a constant balancing act to keep your body upright. The movement of your chest when you breathe, affecting your whole torso to expand and retract. You can feel a tingling on the top of your head; your hair is growing, your nails are growing, your skin is renewing itself from the inside; cells shifting places, from inside to out, until they reach the surface and let go, in the shredding of skin and hair. Everywhere you go you're leaving a dusty trace behind you. Feel the vibration of inter-cellular motion, electrons circulating the nucleus, atoms bouncing off atoms, cells dividing and multiplying. The ongoing life and death, building up and breaking down, of your body.*
>
> Excerpt from *Unsettling I: Schillerplatz* (2017)

SHIFTING OUR ATTENTION TO OUR BODILY SENSES is a form of embodied learning. This means studying, not only as an intellectual process, but as a learning practice where our whole being is involved – our mind, body, emotions, experiences and spirit. Learning from a place where our bodies are recognized as both carriers of knowledge – of experience, memories, habits and skills – and as receivers of knowledge through our different senses.

Embodied learning challenges the Cartesian split that posits that body and mind are distinct and separate entities, stuck in a dualism that puts mind over matter. This figuration still dominates Western thought and practices. It replicates in how we organize our lives; into private vs public, intellectual work vs manual labour, and put these into hierarchies; where public and intellectual work is valued over private and manual labour. In traditional education this mani-

51 Minh-ha, *Woman, Native, Other. Writing Postcoloniality and Feminism.*, 39.

fest as an overt focus on the intellectual development of the student. "Book knowledge", knowledge derived from intellectual work, is valued over experience and skills.

Even in critical and radical pedagogies, there is a tendency to focus on analytic skills and critical reasoning. Though experience is valued, and representation of different bodies and physical identities might be addressed, there is still a discomfort connected with bringing attention to our bodies in the classroom. So much of the pain of oppression resides in our bodies. They remind us of what we have been through, our scars and bruises, and brings to mind how we are being perceived by others. Oppression often reduces us to only being bodies, without agency or intellectual capacity. There is a promise, of the critical classroom, that it will allow us to transcend the body and meet in an equality of the mind.

Still, we recognize what happens when we cross that Cartesian split: knowing something, intellectually, changes when that knowledge is able to land in the body – when we sense and feel that knowledge in our being. Bringing something we know in our bodies to an intellectual level, putting words on our experience, changes that experience, for ourselves and for others. Both mind and body, as non-separate elements, are needed for learning to be profound, and radical – for studying in a way that changes us. Nancy Scheper-Hughes, American professor of Medical Anthropology, writes:

> "The individual body is a given, biopsychological, existential reality. It refers to the processes of becoming and being a person, an embodied self. In this instance, the body is seen as unique, singular, individual, and personally experienced. At the same time, this 'individual' body–conceived as the center of the perceiving, experiencing, thinking world–is always mediated through collective cultural meanings. The self-evident yet contradictory proposition is that humans both have and are bodies. Our bodies are simultaneously objects of and

> subject to our 'selves.' We could say that we are at one and the same time insiders and outsiders to ourselves."[52]

THE EXPERIENCE of both having and being a body are sometimes contradictory. Cultural and political expectations create a clash between how others perceive us, and how we experience ourselves. The language of contemporary Western culture seems to favour having a body as an object that you can weigh and measure, that can work for you and that you can work on, in a way that have us dissociating from our bodies, to the extent that they might end up as an object for us to control. When we feel that we fail in controlling our bodies, it causes room for resentment and actively working to detach from the body. Traumatic events also create dissociation; physical and sexual violence especially forces the need to flee the body and the pain that has been inflicted on it. Both personal and cultural experiences might lead to a relationship to our bodies that is marked by abstraction and fragmentation.

Embodied learning works on reconnecting that bond, to create access to and validation for what we know in our bodies. For pedagogy, this means both recognizing the embodied learning that is always already happening, whether we have intended it or not, and amplifying our attention to embodied knowledge through reminders and exercises.

Meeting in the classroom is not just an intellectual encounter, but a en encountering of bodies. What we say is expressed through our bodily presence, and read through what our bodies represent. Our bodies are ascribed gender and race, class and culture, age and functionality, in more or less immediate and unconscious processes, that affect how what we express is being received. Power plays out as an encountering of bodies, not just as a meeting of minds.

Moreover, our bodies are experienced as a physical presence; reactions move between bodies without necessarily involving the conscious mind. We move around each other, adapt our movement

52 Nancy Scheper-Hughes, "A Finger in the Wound: On Pain, Scars, and Suffering," *Representations* 146, no. 1 (2019): 41.

so everyone can fit, we greet each other not just with words but with our body language. We breathe in different tempo, we move in different ways, we register the mass of other bodies, their smell, their posture, their hand movements, the direction of their gaze, and we interpret meanings in accordance with our experience and learnt behaviour.

When thinking about the role of bodies in pedagogy, it is important to recognize the amount of reports of sexual abuse and misconduct that take place in classrooms. The abrupt experience of being forced to become a sexualized body, a body as object for someone else's desires. When the attention you get shifts, from what knowledge you bring, to the body you are. And the violence that we experience in the rest of society, being replicated between the walls of the classroom. Ignoring the presence and impact of bodies in the classroom, makes us lack in language to describe what has happened to us. Naming the power plays that does not use words – the unwanted touch, intimidation through physical proximity, transgressions without invitation – is part of naming the impact and consequence of bodies in a classroom. These rooms are not exempt from the power imbalances that are reproduced in society and have to be addressed.

Seemingly contradictory, a resistance to acknowledging the body in the classroom can come from a place of wanting to protect the body. The intellectual space of the classroom offers a promise of freedom from having to be a body. It is presented as a place that favours your intellect, where how you look or dress does not matter. This promise resonates with a much desired freedom from having your body considered an object.

In reality, only some people have the privilege of not being considered bodies; of transcending their sweaty, smelly, heavy, pulsating physique and all that it represents. People, whose bodies fit with the expectation of authority and intelligence (white, male), escape the weight of representation. Other bodies, by their mere presence, challenge the institutions that are not accustomed to their presence. As in many classrooms I have been, some bodies cannot even get through the door, because of lack of accessibility measures. bell hooks is a Black American scholar, feminist intellectual and social activist. She writes:

> "The erasure of the body encourages us to think that we are listening to neutral, objective facts, facts that are not particular to who is sharing the information. We are invited to teach information as though it does not emerge from bodies. Significantly, those of us who are trying to critique biases in the classroom have been compelled to return to the body to speak about ourselves as subjects in history. We are all subjects in history. We must return ourselves to a state of embodiment in order to deconstruct the way power has been traditionally orchestrated in the classroom, denying subjectivity to some groups and according it to others. By recognizing subjectivity and limits of identity, we disrupt that objectification that is so necessary in a culture of domination."[53]

BELL HOOKS makes the link from embodiment to subjectivity. Acknowledging how information comes from bodies challenges a Western positivist view on knowledge as objective, and the universalist claims that follow such a position. Attention to bodies brings forth the importance of difference, and of knowledge as partial and plural. Situating knowledge in the bodies that speaks it out loud, situates knowledge in experience and memory, as well as in imagination and creativity.

In an art education context, we encounter a lot of different materials – clay, paint, wood, glass, silk, wool, stone, paper. We see these materials, but we get to know them through the sense of touch and smell, how they sound and feel, how they bend to our touch. We need to use our hands, our arms and legs, our feet and whole body to manipulate material. In these settings, we find another way of being

---

53 bell hooks, *Teaching to Transgress: Education as the Practice of Freedom* (New York,NY: Routledge, 1994), 139.

bodies – the working body, the capable body. This embodiment is less contradictory than the academic one. These classrooms welcome the body, and the teachers are often experts on embodied learning. Not surprisingly, the teachers of tacit knowledge are placed low on the academic scale. These teachers are paid less.

Separating these classrooms, and these types of knowledges, is a mistake. Putting them in a binary opposition is worse. In art education we can pride ourselves in doing both – intellectual work is at play in the workshops, embodied work happens in the theoretical classrooms. There is no gain in separating these, and putting them in hierarchies.

In bell hook's vision of transformative education, the teacher's role is to support the student's strive for wholeness. For her, this includes both body, mind and spirit. When hooks writes about academia, she taps into her own yearning, as a young person, to be whole.

> "Like so many working-class kids coming from families where our parents had not attended college, my vision of what this experience would be like was shaped by an old-fashioned understanding of the intellectual as a being who seeks union of mind, body, and spirit, a union of the intellectual as whole person. Even though I rarely found that understanding affirmed in my academic experience, I continued to work toward this vision of wholeness."[54]

HOOKS' PROPOSITION FOR EDUCATION is not about enforcing an inner life, but maintaining that our inner lives should not be ignored. For her, this falls into the realm of spirituality. hooks insistence on spirituality in the classroom draws from her experience of growing up in a Black community in the U.S in the 1960s, where spirituality was a source of hope as well as a source of resistance

54 bell hooks, *Teaching Community: A Pedagogy of Hope* (New York,NY: Routledge, 2003), 179.

against racist dehumanization. Entering the academy, she experienced how her inherent sense of interconnections that came from spirituality, was at odds with ideas about academic life and how education was framed. Academia favored modes of knowing that honored data, logic, analysis, and a detached objectivity. "Being" was defined by systemic disconnection and disassociation, the individual enforcing its sense of subjectivity through claiming independence.[55]

hooks' understanding of spirituality is that of an identification with experience, rather than submission to a set of scriptures or beliefs. She invites us to have a conversation that spans beyond the strictly academic, to examine our experiences, emotions, desires and beliefs. Her aim is that of collective healing – healing the shadow of our society – in a process that engages the individual, but is held by the community of the classroom. The transformative classroom that hooks presents, is a place "... where paradise can be realized, a place of passion and possibility, a place where spirit matters, where all that we learn and know leads us into greater connection, into greater understanding of life lived in community."[56]

Several decolonial thinkers, like Gloria Anzaldùa, M. Jacqui Alexander and Roxana Ng, make a connection between spirit and embodiment. Contrary to Western beliefs, that put spirituality exclusively in the realm of religion or folk/indigenous tradition, they see spirituality as an essential part of our being and knowing, including in the idea of spirit in both emotion and psyche.[57] We find in their work a critique of how Western feminism (white feminism) has failed to include the spiritual (or Divine) as an aspect of the human experience. When pushing the epistemological shift that includes experience as an essential part of knowledge, and the personal as part of the political, the spiritual continues to be left out.

It is like Western feminism has bought into the idea that spiritu-

---

55 hooks, *Teaching to Transgress: Education as the Practice of Freedom.*

56 hooks, 183.

57 Roxana Ng, "Decolonizing Teaching and Learning Through Embodied Learning: Toward an Integrated Approach," in *Sharing Breath Embodied Learning and Decolonization*, ed. Sheila Batacharya and Yuk-Lin Renita Wong (Edmonton, AU: AU Press, 2018).

ality can only be read as part of the oppressive structure of organized religion and patriarchal tradition, and thus needs to be dismissed.

Importantly, these decolonial thinkers all seem to place the spirit in the body. It is not that transcendent energy, but rather in accordance with the life-giving rhythm of breath – transgressing the body, moving with and through it, but not leaving it behind. Spirituality is in the quotidian habits and rituals, often located to the private sphere of the home – sweeping the floor, washing the clothes, growing plants and cooking food, rhymes and songs associated with everyday tasks. The day to day ceremonies of gratefulness and quiet prayers to the divine. Praise to the small things.

Located in body and flesh, the spirit catches the inter-generational experiences and memories that reside in the body. Echoed in the sacred rituals and ceremonies that are passed on generation to generation, the spiritual is embodied and inscribed in the flesh. These inscription carry the collective knowledge so that it might again be decoded by the community.

> "The purpose of the body is to act not simply, though importantly, as an encasement of the Soul, but also as a medium of Spirit, the repository of a consciousness that derives from a source residing elsewhere, another ceremonial ritual marking. To this end, embodiment functions as a pathway to knowledge, a talking book, whose intelligibility relies on the social – the spiritual expertise of a community to decode Sacred knowledge"[58]

A DECOLONIAL READING OF SPIRITUALITY reminds us how the body is a site of knowledge, that can be read in careful collectivity. Teaching with this in mind, studying holds the possibility of healing. To bell hooks this makes the teacher a healer[59], but I am not sure how to subscribe to this notion, without a better comprehen-

58 M. Jacqui Alexander, *Pedagogies of Crossing: Meditations on Feminism, Sexual Politics, Memory and the Sacred* (Durham and London: Duke University Press, 2005), 325.

59 hooks, *Teaching Community: A Pedagogy of Hope*, 181.

sion of what a healer would be and mean in my specific context. Still, I acknowledge the classroom as a place where healing can happen, and study as a process that can reconnect gaps and wounds, if we support and encourage this path.

How we relate to the future unknown

The future is always unknown to us. But at times, change happens more rapidly, and the future seems more immanently present. Our relationship to the future changes in the face of catastrophe. Uncertainty makes us unsure of how to respond. What do we dream about when the future seems so bleak? How do we relate to the future when we cannot make plans? How do we study for a future unknown?

Cultural-political geographer Ben Anderson has managed to map different ways we relate to the future and how we make futures present. The future is not only connected to the present through a relation of succession. Nor is the future "...only a mystery to be waited for, a not-yet that gives hope, or a virtuality to become worthy of. It may be all these, but the future is also present while remaining absent – whether that be in models, expectations, scenarios, hopes, or in countless other ways."[60]

The future incubates within the present, that is, the seeds to both life and disaster can be found in life as it is. Disaster is also emergent – it changes as it develops and circulates, and the outcomes are often unforeseeable. It takes an enormous effort to analyse the interdependencies, flows and circulations that impact how the future plays out.

Anderson investigates how existing power relations are being protected from change by looking into the work of anticipatory action from governments and their organizations, and the policies and programs that are put in place to deal with catastrophic futures

60 Ben Anderson, "Preemption, Precaution, Preparedness: Anticipatory Action and Future Geographies," *Progress in Human Geography*, 2010, 793. In this quote Andersson makes reference to Nikolas S. Rose, Powers of freedom: reframing political thought (Cambridge: Cambridge University Press, 1999), Ben Anderson. Transcending without transcendence: utopianism and an ethos of hope (Antipode 38, 691–710, 2006), J.D. Dewsbury, Unthinking subjects: Alain Badiou and the event of thought in thinking politics (Transactions of the Institute of British Geographers NS 32, 443–59, 2007)

– with terrorism, pandemics, natural disasters and climate change. As a threat to liberal-democratic life, and capitalism "anticipatory action aims to ensure that no bad surprises happen"[61]. By predicting the future, based on archival and statistical reasoning, and identify any threats to the existing social order, anticipatory action is put in place by governments to protect what fits within the parameters of, what Anderson calls, "valued life".

> "...anticipatory action is now imbricated with the plurality of power relations that make up contemporary liberal democracies. This means that any type of anticipatory action will only provide relief, or promise to provide relief, to a valued life, not necessarily all of life. Certain lives may have to be abandoned, damaged or destroyed in order to protect, save or care for life."[62]

THESE PREDICTIONS become justifications for political actions in the present. We can see how it influences migration politics, labour rights, investments in infrastructure, social planning etc. The categorization of whose lives are to be considered valued and whose are not, will not be publicly articulated. Instead, these sacrifices are presented as unavoidable – hard, but necessary – claiming to be on the side of what is universally good for humanity. Anderson asks us to pay attention to how anticipatory action protects the current systems and power in place, at the cost of the lives of those who are not valued by those systems.

How might we want to relate to the future differently? Looking to the work of social movements, Anderson found practices of imagining the future that do not aim to predict and contain what is coming. He looks mainly at performative practices in the form of climate change scenarios that stage several different futures for the participants to experience, in a range between the utopian and the dysto-

61 Anderson, 782.
62 Anderson, 780.

pian. The workshops allow for participants to experience how different scenarios function, and their emotional response to them, without disclosing their probability. Anderson introduces the notion of *the future as a surprise*, as an open set of endless possibilities.

> "First, disclosing the future as a surprise means that one cannot then predetermine the form of the future by offering a deterministic prediction. Instead, the future as surprise can only be rendered actionable by knowing a range of possible futures that may happen, including those that are improbable. Second, statements about the future as a surprise do not enable the future to be grasped and handled through a process of induction from the past distribution of events. Instead, anticipatory action must be based on a constant readiness to identify another possible way in which a radically different future may play out."[63]

IN ANDERSON'S REASONING THE FUTURE is in many ways unknowable, it is not a lack of knowledge that we can simply overcome. We cannot draw any linear predictions from what we have experienced so far. Instead, we have to find ways to handle the contingency of life by a constant readiness for a future that is always changing into radically different forms. Accepting how the future will surprise us, allows us to practice staying with uncertainty. We can put our efforts into imagining both probable and improbable futures, paying attention to what is incubated within the present, and foster a state of readiness. The future as a surprise offers a shift in how we relate to the unknown that does not aim to control, but with an element of welcoming that includes a possible opening.

Education makes the future present, in the sense that we tend to study *for* something. Education is often prescribed as preparation – for a successful career in a future society, for novel research, or for making art that will reflect the state of the world. Education is to a

63 Anderson, 782.

large degree built on prediction and the idea that the students can become prepared for the future they are stepping into. In uncertain times, the promise of education to prepare and adequately equip students for the future becomes harder to fulfil. What promises can we offer when we do not know what we are teaching and studying for?

Roland Barnett, Emeritus Professor of Higher Education at the University of London, suggests we should teach being-with-uncertainty. In a paper from 2004, Barnett poses the question "What is it to learn for an unknown future?" sparked by the complex relationship to knowledge that informs today's Western universities. Due to information overload (from a growing multitude of entities in the world) combined with the speed at which the world is changing, knowledge has become marked by fragmentation, fragility, fluidity and complexity. It is too much to collectively comprehend, to the extent that our interpretations of the world are at ends with each other. Barnett names this situation *supercomplexity.*[64]

In contrast to complexity, which can be unravelled, figured out and found a solution for, supercomplexity can never be resolved. It calls everything we know into question. In response, academia tends to ask open textured questions (addressing a global and plural world), that in turn yield a multitude of answers and further questions. Supercomplexity multiplies the differences in interpretations, until we are in a situation where "... we never could hope satisfactorily even to describe the world, let alone act with assuredness in it."[65] This leads to an inner sense of a destabilized world. What is being questioned by supercomplexity is not only our knowledge or skills, but our being.

What is specific about these times is not that the world changes, but the character and intensity of these changes, that "bare in upon our sense of our own being; they are, in sum, ontological challenges."[66] Barnett detects the need for an ontological shift in higher education, that puts knowledge and skills in the background, to centre

---

64 Roland Barnett, "Learning for an Unknown Future," *Higher Education Research & Development* 23, no. 3 (2004).

65 Barnett, 250.

66 Barnett, 249.

being. In face of supercomplexity, Barnett proposes the need for a high-risk pedagogy, "a pedagogy for human being", that teaches students how to deal with uncertainty, with the questions that cannot be solved, and with gaps that cannot be bridged.

> " It is a learning for an unknown future that enables the self to come to understand and strengthen itself, much as it recognizes that there is always a gap between that self-awareness and the need to act in the world. Part, therefore, of such a learning is acquiring the capacity to live with the existential angst that derives from an awareness of the gap between one's actions and one's limited grounds for those actions. Understood this way, a pedagogy for an unknown future becomes a pedagogy with the unknown built into it as living principles of educational exchanges and accomplishments."[67]

BEING-WITH-UNCERTAINTY is characterised by an openness to knowing the world through epistemological gaps. This means recognizing that we will not be able to act with certainty in this world, while still managing to not become paralysed by this insight. Furthermore, we must learn not simply to act, but to act with intent, despite the lack of guarantees for a desired outcome.

A pedagogy for being-with-uncertainty must itself be informed by this premise, which means the teacher must be able to teach without the need to proclaim certainty. This entails being able to teach with open pedagogical frames, from a place of humility towards the limits of one's knowledge, and without guarantees for the outcome one has planned for. It demands of the teacher to be vulnerable, to not shield themselves behind certainty, in order to meet in that space of radical openness, where one is willing to change and be changed by an other[68]. The ontological shift, from an emphasis on knowing

---

67 Barnett, 260.
68 hooks, *Teaching Community: A Pedagogy of Hope*, 192.

to an emphasis on being, entails showing up as full human beings, as persons, sharing not only what we know but who we are. This is a demanding and vulnerable process.

As a response to Anderson's introduction of the future as a surprise, coupled with Barnett's call for teaching being-with-uncertainty, I think about the possibilities to teach and to study for readiness. Readiness implicates an active state, that fosters being present, focusing on the here and now, paying attention to what is happening as it unfolds. It does not shy away from the future unknown through passivity or escapism, nor does it try to predict and control what is coming. Readiness implicates an acceptance of the limits of our knowledge, without a passive or reactionary stance. Readiness can relate to the unknown through an attentive presence and a radical openness, rather than through certainty and control.

If we study for readiness, we welcome the future as a surprise. In contrast to anticipatory action, that is looking to predict the future and act to prevent anything unexpected to happen, we expect change. We are ready for the change that is coming, even though we do not know how it will surprise us. A pedagogy of readiness asks us to take the risk of uncertainty, and to find ways to deal with being in an unsettled state.

Let go of control.

Shake the walls of reality until all is a blur.

You are breaking up. You are de-connecting, re-connecting.

Something over-and-done with will come back to you. The un-familiar will come into view. Your blind spot will

re-focus. You will see outside of yourself.

You need to start moving. Something needs to be done. It is in your hands.

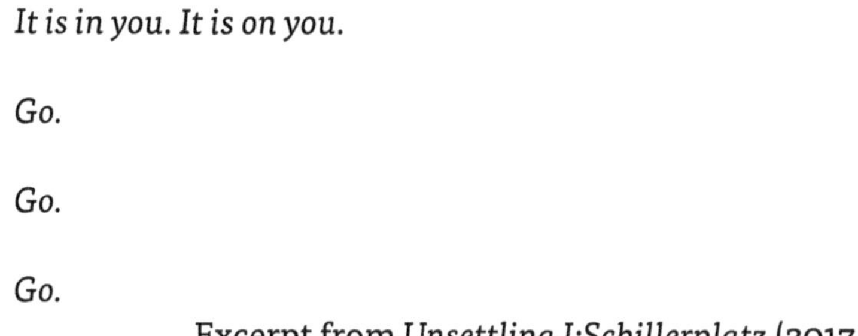

It is in you. It is on you.

Go.

Go.

Go.

Excerpt from *Unsettling I:Schillerplatz* (2017)

READINESS ACTIVATES THE PRESENT. It does not ignore the now for later. To be ready is to be present in the moment, and to pay attention to how the future incubates within the present; alert to the way the tide turns, the earth shifts, the wind moves. Allowing time to move through us, like a stream, a breeze or a wave.

Readiness is the knowledge of Black people and POCs in white supremacy, of queers in heterosexual hegemony, of women in patriarchy, of indigenous people on colonized land. It is the knowledge of how to navigate in a hostile world, of constant proximity to erratic violence, of adaptation, of vulnerability, of resilience and the knowledge that everything will change and change is both fast and slow, big and small. It is the survival tactic that people caught between worlds cultivate.[69]

Studying for readiness, we practice how to hold on; how to keep breathing, keep growing, living, listening, despite the pain and proximity to death and decomposition. To be able to trust and make this shift in attention – from preparing for a future, to be ready for the unknown to surprise us – we will have to rely on each other, in mutual dependency. Readiness demands being able to love, to keep on loving as the world hardens. To refuse competition, control and borders when scarcity hits. Readiness demands being in living relation with others, with community, with the world.

To educate for readiness, is to offer access to a state of adaptation, of flexibility, and the strength that comes from vulnerability. To find ways to hold a space that allows us to be vulnerable, soft and pliant,

69 Anzaldúa, *Borderlands/La Frontera: The New Mestiza*, 61.

mouldable and strong. A state that allows us to bend, but not break. A state of readiness demands good condition, exercise, repetition, upkeep, without particular progression or end goal. Readiness has no finish line. It is a state of becoming, rather than a place of arrival.

Teaching and studying without guarantees

Now that we have paved the way for a shift, from utopia towards the unknown, through being-with-uncertainty and studying for readiness, this process needs to be supplemented with an ethical and political grounding. No longer relying on utopia to imagine otherwise, we need to find other ways to strengthen our intentions towards the future. How can we stay accountable, responsible and examine our complicity, in the face of the unknown?

Pedagogies of the unknown cannot be a cart blanche for everything goes. With the release of our urge to control the future, there might come a sense of relief in letting go – a sense that a burden has been lifted. But we cannot allow ourselves to rest too comfortably in that ease. Our future is still very much at risk. Pedagogies of the unknown must find their ethical grounding – to hold responsibility and accountability as well as political intent.[70] The space that has opened up with the shift towards the unknown must be considered carefully, and moved through in a way that honours the change we want to see in the world.

I am bringing in Spivak's theory of the double bind because it captures the experience of carrying the unknown close to heart. She manages to capture the intensity and tension of an inescapable position, where however we turn it seems to put us at a dead end. At the same time, she provides us with an ethical opening, a possibility to act, and to do so with intention.

> "Radical alterity – the wholly other – must be thought and must be thought through imaging. To be born human is to be born angled toward an other and

70 For me, this entails holding on to an intersectional feminist politics; insisting on holding the power relations of race-class-gender-sexuality etc. in mindful tension.

> others. To account for this the human being presupposes the quite-other. This is the bottom line of being-human as being-in-the-ethical-relation. By definition, we cannot – no self can – reach the quite-other. Thus the ethical situation can only be figured in the ethical experience of the impossible. This is the founding gap in all act or talk, most especially in acts or talk that we understand to be closest to the ethical – the historical and the political. We will not leave the historical and the political behind. We must somehow attempt to supplement the gap." [71]

TO UNDERSTAND THE DOUBLE BIND, we must begin with the ethical relation, the human in relation to the other. Spivak's ethics is based on being together in difference, while accepting that one can never fully understand the other as well as one self. Still, one needs to find a way to be in ethical relationship with one another. We make assumptions about each other, while knowing we can never really know if what we presuppose is accurate. She calls this the ethical angle, or "othering".

This is the basis for the ethical as an experience of the impossible. There is a gap between our intentions and what is possible to achieve from those intentions. There is no ethical practice that can close this gap – we can only supplement it as persistently as possible, without any guarantees, in knowing the impossibility to fully realize the ethical. This is the double bind of the ethical relation.

Spivak gets the term double bind from Gregory Bateson, who identified it as a communication paradox in families inflicted by schizophrenia, but later admitted it to be relevant to all people. In its original use, the term marks not simply a contradiction or a conflict between two utterances, but a demand that in its intricacy is impossible to fulfil or escape. Whatever response you give, whatever choice you make, you will fail – you are damned if you do, and damned if you don't.

---

71 Spivak, *An Aesthetic Education in the Era of Globalization*, 97–98.

Importantly, there is also an element of authority in this equation. The one imposing the double bind is usually an authority figure, like a parent, a doctor or a teacher; someone who one is dependent on, and who one does not question. There is also an element of confusion in how the double bind is imposed; it is usually hard for the subject to describe the nature of the double bind, and therefore to question it. The message is transferred on different levels of abstraction, through implications, tone of voice, body-language, and can be made in a combination of explicit and implicit language. The contradictions of the double bind can be hidden in layers of communication.

Spivak displaces the term double bind from its origin position as an issue in relationships between individuals, to be used in lager socio-political contexts. She uses it to describe the binding relationship between the global North and the global South that is globalisation, as well as the conflicting consequences of the Enlightenment forming the base for the humanities of today. The double bind is a recurring sentiment that she applies to a range of different relations, from the inter-personal to the political.

> "When we find ourselves in the subject position of two determinate decisions, both right (or both wrong), one of which cancels the other, we are in an aporia which by definition cannot be crossed, or a double bind. Yet, it is not possible to remain in an aporia or a double bind. It is not a logical or philosophical problem like a contradiction, a dilemma, a paradox, an antinomy. It can only be described as an experience. It discloses itself in being crossed. For, as we know every day, even by supposedly not deciding, one of those two right or wrong decisions gets taken, and the aporia or double bind remains."[72]

72 Spivak, 104.

A DOUBLE BIND is marked by the undecidable in every decision. In the double bind, the possibility – or impossibility – to decide, still comes with the burden of responsibility. Whether we choose to make a decision or not, a decision will be made. There is no escaping the situation. Spivak suggests that in spite of the impossibility of making it "right" we must honour this responsibility, and keep working on supplementing the gap.

My suggestion is that we consider our relation to the unknown as a series of double binds. The experience of needing to engage with the future, even though we have no possibility to predict what it will be, much less act with certainty towards it. The experience of wanting to teach for the change we want to see in the world, without falling into the many traps of relying on linear predictions from what we already know. The experience of needing to let go of hope, yet relying on hope to fuel the fight for a future. The experience of urgency in the face of catastrophe, yet resisting the urge to make quick decisions out of certainty.

The double bind is more than a contradiction. It is an experience of being caught in the tension between two opposing poles, without any possibility to escape. Every suggestion comes with objections, but no solutions. It is irresolvable. This brings us to a state of loss, of confusion and puzzlement.

So what is to be done when caught in this inescapable state? Vanessa de Oliveira Andreotti has reformulated the task of learning the double bind as "Learning (to play) the double bind (rather than to solve it)."[73] The figure of the double bind is not static, it is moving. Spivak attests to it the swing of a pendulum, moving between the two ends of a spectrum. This movement denies neither, emphasizing both, in a "a series of balances ending in play"[74]. Andreotti sees the constant balancing act of holding both ends of the double bind in tension "with their potential negative and positive aspects in view

---

73 Vanessa de Oliveira Andreotti, "Spivak: Overview of Critique and Educational Propositions (Bergamo)," 3, accessed September 26, 2018, https://www.academia.edu/4777864/Spivak_overview_of_critique_and_educational_propositions_Bergamo_.

74 Spivak, *An Aesthetic Education in the Era of Globalization*, 16.

(and being aware of the partiality of this view)"[75] as a site of play. To play is to learn how to stay in the tension of the double bind, without being paralyzed by it.

Andreotti describes the complexities that come with this task. Realizing how dialectic negotiations often end up getting caught in opposition, in a reflection of what was opposed in the first place, replicating an oppressive system without being able to escape it. In Spivak's work, there is no uncontaminated position, no place of innocence, no pure solutions, no tool or concept or weapon that cannot be turned against us. Both ends of the dialectic are part of the double bind[76].

Spivak offers evidence for the conflicting, and often exhausting, feelings that comes with navigating the ethical and puts us in the middle of tension. Recognizing that the pervasiveness of the double bind can grind us down. The encouragement to play is not an easy, but a necessary one. Playing the double bind is in part accepting the impossibility to get out of it, while still working to supplement the ethical gap. It is a troubled practice that keeps us accountable, recognizing that there is no uncontaminated position to uphold. It is working *despite* impossibility. To do it, still.

Play suggests there is movement built in to the tension of the double bind. I think of it as dancing the tight rope, playing the strings of an instrument, weaving between the threads of the warp, the metal string that cuts through clay, painting on the tension of the canvas. A way of finding movement in between, and on top of, tension. To creatively interpret our situation on, in and in between the mere rational or reasonable. This is where aesthetic education carries a promise.

What can happen when we apply the notion of playing the double bind to pedagogies of the unknown? Can we define the inescapable double bind that holds us accountable, or in relation, when we engage in practices of imagination? And how can they be a site of play?

The double bind of imagining otherwise stretches between insist-

75 Andreotti, "Spivak," 4.
76 Andreotti, 4.

ing on a future and the need to ignore it. Playing the double bind implies examining this experience, and finding out what is moving, or movable, between the ends of the pendulum – of striving and working towards change while practising to stay present, attentive and allow for hesitation. Of allowing ourselves hopelessness and despair, to see what comes beyond those states. Of imagining better futures while knowing they will disappoint. These double binds move us, slowly, from utopia towards the unknown.

Towards the future without guarantees

The works I have cited in this chapter are not very optimistic. They have in common that their proposals for dealing with the future unknown comes without guarantees. Although change of unjust systems is a very present driving force in these writers' work, they show no strong conviction that the change they believe is needed will come. The future bears as much death as it bears life; they will not let us ignore one or the other.

Their thinking is without prediction for the future, it does not prepare us as much as it offers us work to do. They show us possible places to start, but do not show us to where we will end up. They come with urgency, but the process suggested is often slow, persistent, in the grinding work of the everyday. They urge us on with glimpses of *we must*, in the forms of hard work and inconvenient effort. They refuse to offer us any satisfaction in righting the wrongs or reconciling our past for a hopeful future.

Still, they are invested in the future and believe in the power of imagination to change society and life on this Earth. What I get from these thinkers is an acknowledgment of the double binds that come with imagining the future. They help me to let go of unexamined hope, to learn to stay with the troubles of a radical imagination, without guarantees. They offer me an opening to the unknown via an imagination that is attentive to change, to all the complex and contaminated aspects of life, without trying to predict what is coming. This future unknown carries no promise.

II: EXPERIMENTING WITH GUIDED MEDITATIONS AS PEDAGOGY

Let me share what I have been up to. Let me introduce you to my practice and how I got interested in pedagogies of the unknown. We will start out in lecture-performance and the inclination to shape shift with a bear, before we dive into the guided meditations. I will summon a hypnotherapist to help us grasp the trance state and decipher the nature of suggestions. I will present to you some key functions of guided meditations, like shifting attention, unsettling and embodied learning, in and out of the classroom. I suggest we hold space for resistance. As we examine the role of the guide and the teacher, I will pass on this role to you.

Access to another state of mind

As teaching has grown more integral to my artistic practice, giving lectures or public presentations has become a returning feature of my work. Dissatisfied with the one-way direction of the lecture format, I started experimenting with how to better engage and activate the audience. I began to emphasize the performative aspects, trying to be very precise in how and to whom the text was presented. I started treating the lecture as a script to be performed; carefully rehearsing each aspect of the text, thinking about tempo and body language. The lectures have become more site specific and intentional in how they address the room and the audience.

Subsequently, I started to add participatory aspects in the form of short exercises mixed in with the lecture, where the audience is asked to do a short writing exercise in response to a question, to move their body and observe how it feels, or to talk to each other about a given subject. These additions are sometimes challenging, both to the audience and to the hosting institutions, pushing at the boundaries of what is expected in a given situation.

These lectures can be understood in the tradition of *lecture-performance*. Central to lecture-performance is the idea of *teaching as art*, that is, considering teaching itself as a central component of the artwork. Lecture-performance tends to blur the lines separating art from discourse about art, and to push past the boundaries of disciplines[77]. The genealogy of lecture-performance can be traced in relation to the larger question of the educational turn in contemporary art, as is done by artist and writer Kristina Lee Podesva, starting from Joseph Beuys' scores of educational lectures and social sculptures, via the institutional critique of Fred Wilson and Andrea Fraser, to the relational aesthetics of the 90s[78], and the self-organized educational initiatives of the 2000s.

Lecture-performance often contains an element of institutional

77 Patricia Milder, "TEACHING AS ART The Contemporary Lecture-Performance," *PAJ: A Journal of Performance and Art* 1, no. 33 (2010): 13–27.

78 Kristina Lee Podesva, "A Pedagogical Turn: Brief Notes on Education as Art," Fillip, 2007, https://fillip.ca/content/a-pedagogical-turn.

critique[79]. The pedagogy of art museums usually takes the form of texts, booklets, guided tours, lectures, and creative workshops directed at children. It comes with the explicit claim to make art more accessible, but will just as often, intentionally or unintentionally, play the part of conserving the separation between those who know, and those who do not. Overly zealous explanations of the art reveal a distrust in the audience own interpretations, deeming their frame of reference invalid. In lecture-performance, the artist uses traditional formats of art pedagogy like educational lectures (Beuys) and guided tours (Fraser), but breaks with the expectations that come with these formats. The performer often exaggerates the tone and address, making it appear ridiculous, or intervene with subjective, subversive or outrageous material. They make visible the institutional structures and simultaneously play with the hierarchies of knowledge – who is in a position to *explain* the art? – bringing attention to how institutions perform their role as public educators and as upholders of certain values (national/liberal/Western etc.).

In my work, the challenge to the institutions has manly consisted of breaking with expected formats, transgressing the traditional boundaries between presenter and audience, by asking of the audience to participate. I have brought attention to the space, the bodies in the space, and the conditions for us being here together, pointing out structural difference and the institution's failure to accommodate difference. I have also allowed myself to be overly emotional, to feel the things I have presented, both laughing and crying, pausing when needed and raised my voice in exclamation.

My very first attempt at including a guided meditation in a lecture, was in the setting of an academic conference called "Exploring the Animal Turn" in Lund, in the spring of 2014[80]. I wanted to find a way to address and engage the public in a more intimate way than I could with a lecture. The lecture I presented was on shape shifting in Swedish and Sami folk culture, and came out of my recent experience of of late-night hallucinations while breastfeeding my baby.

---

79 Milder, "TEACHING AS ART The Contemporary Lecture-Performance."

80 "Exploring the Animal Turn," accessed October 11, 2021, https://www.pi.lu.se/en/publications/pufendorf-ias-publications/exploring-animal-turn.

Being constantly awakened at night, I would try some of the relaxation techniques that I practiced while preparing for giving birth, in an effort to relax and get back to sleep. They were simple techniques of slow, deep breathing and focused attention to the body, that I found in books and articles on pregnancy and labor[81]. For my delivery they failed miserably, but for relaxing and getting into a half sleep state, while breastfeeding at night, they worked. They stopped my thoughts from spinning and calmed me down, saving me a lot of energy, and helped me to stay relaxed.

Falling in and out of sleep, sensations of my body started to morph and take more and more vivid forms. After experiencing the dysmorphia of pregnancy I was already in an unsettled state; my body growing and expanding, life appropriating my body and extending into the world in a way I had little control over, senses introverted, a presence intense and energetic pushing at my inner organs, feet tickling my groin, a spine pressing visibly through my skin. Followed by the violent separation, the mitosis, the cutting open of my midsection and the following month of re-connecting the upper and lower halves of my body. I had to find new ways to be in and with my body, to re-establish trust and build a new relationship; everything I knew about my body open for change, transformation, morphing, separating and re-connecting. Much less scary than it sounds, but life and mind altering, never the less.

This unsettled state opened me up for experiences I might have else resisted or rejected. The night sessions started to take life. Every night I would shape shift into this bear; starting with the nose, following the air up my nostrils down my mouth where teeth and taste had changed. I could feel my nose and mouth as a snout, and my body heavy and robust, as *I was the bear*. It was a calming, yet powerful, experience.

From my childhood occupation with fantasy and science fiction, I always dreamed of being able to shape shift. Inspired by the *The Dark Is Rising Sequence* by Susan Cooper I practiced concentration in

81 Susanna Heli, *Föda Utan Rädsla* (Stockholm: Bonnier Existens, 2009).

my room late at night[82]. Focusing on visualizing every detail of the animal I wanted to become. Sometimes my efforts extended into my dreams, but that was it. No changes that I experienced as "real". This time it was a bit different. The experience was enticing, and I began to seek it out, to follow the same path night after night, trying to expand this in-between state, this place of becoming, where my body could be more than human. Furthermore, I could *make* my body more than human, by concentration and relaxation, with a radical openness and attentiveness, I could change, shift and shape the world in a new way. I felt as if I could *become with* the bear. As my body changed, so did my relation to the immediate surroundings and the world. I was resting, sensing, smelling, tasting differently. My experience of the world changed as my senses developed. As an artist, this process was of great interest to me.

The trance state

Meditation can help bring us to a state of trance. According to Milton H Erickson, American psychiatrist who specialized in medical hypnosis, the concept of trance is not something extra-ordinary. It is the equivalent of daydreaming, staring out the window, or the flow that comes from intense exercise or creative work[83]. It is a state that we, under the right conditions, can access by ourselves.

> " In the hypnotic state subjects are open to ideas. They like to examine ideas in terms of their memories, their conditionings and all of the various experimental learnings of life. They take your suggestion and translate that into their own body learnings."[84]

---

82 Susan Cooper, *The Dark Is Rising Sequence* (Margret K. McElderry Books, 2013).

83 Milton H Erickson and Ernest L Rossi, "Two-Level Communication and the Microdynamics of Trance and Suggestion," *The American Journal of Clinical Hypnosis, Reprinted in Collected Papers Vol.1*, 1976, 18.

84 Ernest L Rossi, *The Nature of Hypnosis and Suggestion. The Collected Papers of Milton H. Erickson on Hypnosis, Volume 1* (New York, NY: Halsted Press, 1980), 1663.

THE TRANCE STATE is interesting, in a pedagogical sense, because it is an adaptive state[85], "a state of increased awareness and responsiveness to ideas"[86]. It opens a path to the unconscious, giving us a chance to take a look at those deep-set ideas and beliefs about ourselves and the world that we do not usually access, or question. It has the potential to help us break with old patterns and change our habits.

Erickson trusted that people, in their own natural history, have the resources to overcome the problem for which they are seeking help. Consequently, the adaptive state is not a place to enforce something new, in the sense of adding new knowledge, but it opens us up to remember what we did not know we had forgotten. It might be knowledges that we have suppressed or ignored. "A trance only allows you to handle all the learning you have already acquired."[87]

The role of the hypnotherapist is to find ways of inducing a trance state and to guide the client through the experience of hypnosis, by presenting them with verbal input in the form of suggestions. Suggestions can be defined as statements intended to provoke both cognitive and sensory emotional responses. Similar to everyday verbal communication, suggestions are ideas or proposals that depend on both direct and indirect speech, carrying both symbolic and more direct meaning.

By accepting or rejecting the invitations presented to them, the client is always in control of the journey. In this sense, hypnosis is always a matter of self-hypnosis. In contrast to the popular image of hypnosis as a manipulative and intrusive act, that puts the client totally out of control, modern day hypnotherapy relies on a willingness from the client to put themselves in a trance state.[88]

---

85 John Webber and RJ Thomas, "Talking Therapy Ep. 28 Dr. Jeffrey Zeig on the Evolution of Psychotherapy," accessed December 5, 2019, http://www.talkingtherapypodcast.com/.

86 Milton H Erickson, "Pediatric Hypnotherapy," *The American Journal of Clinical Hypnosis, Reprinted in Collected Papers Vol.4*, 1958, 729.

87 Sidney Rosen, *My Voice Will Go with You: The Teaching Tales of Milton H. Erickson* (New York, NY and London,UK: W.W. Norton and Company, Inc., 1991), 79.

88 Webber and Thomas, "Talking Therapy Ep. 28 Dr. Jeffrey Zeig on the Evolution of Psychotherapy." According to Jeffrey K Zeig, Erickson's methods are less didactic and more performative than traditional therapy, in service of setting a climate for therapy where self-hypnosis is possible.

Guiding a meditation is similar in the sense that it consists of a series of suggestions that can be accepted or rejected by the participant. They can take the form of instructions (direct as in "close your eyes" or more indirect as in "let your breath touch your heart"), or the form of scenes and scenarios ("the floor beneath you is connected to the walls" or "on the surface of Gaia there is a house"). They can be more or less open to interpretation, and more or less challenging as well.

It is not easy to discern the quality of a good suggestion. It is somewhere between the prosaic and the poetic. The balance between being distinct enough to engage with, yet open enough to adapt in accordance with the participants' different experiences. The aim is to have the participants engage with the suggestions, to take them in and react to them. The suggestions are generally repeated in different forms to attract different people's interest. Similar to classroom teaching, where we try to present the same content in a multitude of ways, so that as many students as possible will be able to engage with the material.

I have found inspiration by listening to hundreds of guided meditations, mainly on Insight Timer[89], a community based app that allows users to upload and share meditation content of various genres and quality. Worth mentioning is Jennifer Piercy, a sleep educator and yoga nidra guide, who is devoted to the healing powers of rest, sleep and dreaming[90]. In her work, she manages to share information about the biology of rest and sleep, while offering the possibility to practice relaxation and sleep techniques. Communicating that there is research and experience behind her words, helps to create trust in her guidance. I found her suggestions to be very precise in their formulations, giving a sense that every word counts, and leads you to an opening, a possibility or a connection.

The language I have used in my guided meditations is mainly permissive and affirmative. A lot of the suggestions are written in a language that invites the participant to a practice, rather than instructing them. Verbs like "notice", "search for", "study" and "wit-

89 "Insight Timer - #1 Free Meditation App for Sleep, Relax & More," accessed October 11, 2021, https://insighttimer.com/.

90 Jennifer Piercy's work is available at https://www.sacredsleepyoga.com

ness" bring attention to something in or around the participant. Verbs like "allow yourself", "let go of", "let yourself" and "appreciate" invite the participant to make a step in a direction that they might have felt hindered from. This language is meant to ease the transition, to clear the path in a way that makes movement possible, and to confirm the participant's needs and desires. Affirmative language, in contrast to authoritative statements, stands as a confirmation of the participant's experience and knowledge, affirming that what they need to know is already there for them to be noticed.

With that said, the guided meditations I have written are not very comfortable or reassuring. They all contain an element of unsettling. The dramaturgy follows an inverted curve, in the form of a bowl. It starts by going inwards and downwards; through noticing our breathing and how our bodies respond, we shift attention from our heads to our bodies below the neck. This process involves a slowing down, with the aim to gather our focus and attention, allowing ourself to disregard the outside world for a moment. This is followed by an awakening of the senses, activating both an awareness of how our body feels, and of the different ways our body is connected to our immediate surroundings. Gradually, this awareness is expanded, out from the room we are in, identifying the connections step-by-step to the bigger world around us.

Discomfort usually arrives when realizing how these connections are flawed. We might feel uncomfortable in our own skin, unsure of how to interpret our body's responses, and let down by its limitations or by the pain that it stores. We might not feel at home with the people around us, distrusting the structures that are supposed to hold us, or betrayed by the community or society that claims our belonging. Confronted by the vastness of the world can have us struck by an almost overwhelming sense of vertigo, and our connection to the world may seem fragmented and incomplete.

Examining our connections to our surroundings reveals all the ways they have been obstructed, interrupted or broken. This is not a comfortable place to rest. The foundation of separation that governs our day-to-day lives becomes unsettled. There is a comfort in separating ourselves and compartmentalizing the troubles of the world, relying on hierarchies to keep things in their place. The separation of body from mind, of our lives from the lives of others, of our biology from that of the natural world, of reason from imagination etc. Though we may not agree with this separation on an intellectual level, there is still some comfort in the systems we recognize. Challenging them brings discomfort.

In this place of discomfort, we practice how to stay and how to play. How to hold on, keep on breathing, keep on listening. Allowing for pain to be real and relational.

This, is where the hard work begins
We ask you to tap into the vulnerability
of living
and dying
together on this damaged earth

To bare your wounds
in this salty sea
and let your scars soften
for a chance
to build new tissue
Use your body's deep memory
as the rooted system
for a new limb to take form
a new, boneless arm
a feeler
extended
with the wisdom
that comes from being hurt

This new tissue
is soft and pink
raw and sensitive
alive

absorb nutrition
brought to you by deep sea currents
from the death and decomposition
of unnamed relatives
connecting across the continental rift
you share this nourishing womb
with most life
on this earth

let your new feeler grow
with the empathic pattern
that comes from knowing each other
in vulnerability
and pain
the necessary connection
of living
body-to-body

Excerpt from *FEELERS* (2018)

THE MESSAGES WE RECEIVE in this adaptable state are not necessarily those we want to hear. Adapting to the world is painful, as this exercise in breathing under water tries to show. It takes effort to make new connections between ourselves and the world. It takes practice to break with the patterns we rely on to form other habits.

To be unsettled is an uneasy feeling of being disturbed, moved, pushed, shaken up or destabilized. Being unsettled from one's position by something or someone is a feeling that lingers, that is not easy to shake off. Being unsettled does not easily re-settle. It is the experience of being pushed out of one position into another, to be moved a bit off center or off the beaten path and getting a slight change in perspective. It can make you lose your bearings, and leave you questioning. It can be a first step in unlearning.

Inserting unsettling elements in the guided meditations is an attempt at practising being-with-uncertainty. To practice staying with what is uncomfortable and allow it to be, without immediately trying to fix things. Exploring how those unsettled feelings rise and fall in a setting that is not too demanding.

Through unsettling, the guided meditations can also help us train our imagination. As an example, the suggestion "let your breath touch your heart" activates our creative mind[91]. The suggestion is unsettling in the sense that it does not match with our biology – our airways and lungs are not directly connected to the heart, so there is no possibility of "touch" in the literal sense of the word. The suggestion is puzzling and confusing, and this glitch in logic provides an opening to think and make connections beyond mere reason. An element of confusion can activate the imagination.

It takes effort to make the connection between the breath and the heart. We cannot simply rely on instant logic, but will have to dig a bit deeper. Our minds will look for connections, or it will create them. In hypnotherapy it is believed that a confused person has their conscious mind busy and occupied, and is therefore inclined

91 Jennifer Piercy, "Bone Deep Sleep | Insight Timer," accessed October 12, 2021, https://insighttimer.com/jenniferpiercy/guided-meditations/bone-deep-sleep.
The suggestion "let your breath touch your heart" is quoted from from Jennifer Piercy's guided meditation "Bone Deep Sleep"

to draw upon unconscious learnings to make sense of things. Instead of analysing we draw on our embodied experience, our suppressed memories, and our creative minds. From there several connections can be made; there is symbolic connections to be made between breath – life – heart – love; a chemical connection, following how oxygen moves through the body; a musical connection, matching the rhythm of the breath with the rhythm of the heart etc.

Readiness (here, present, ready)

> " What we have been ordered to forget is not the capacity to pay attention, but the art of paying attention. If there is an art, and not just a capacity, this is because it is a matter of learning and cultivating, that is to say, making ourselves pay attention. Making in the sense that attention here is not related to that which is defined as a priori worthy of attention, but as something that creates an obligation to imagine, to check, to envisage, consequences that bring into play connections between what we are in the habit of keeping separate. In short, making ourselves pay attention in the sense that attention requires knowing how to resist the temptation to separate what must be taken into account and what may be neglected. "[92]

ISABELLE STENGERS, Belgian philosopher of science, highlights in this quote how shifting attention has to do with making a change to what is worth paying attention to. It can be a way to resist where we are expected to put our energy (on personal progress, individualized success and other capitalist longings, or on mindless distraction, entertaining spectacles and misdirected fears) and a political act of acknowledging what happens in the margins of society; to ideological shifts masked as progress, to wrong doings in plain sight, or to populations and histories that are being ignored.

---

92 Stengers, *In Catastrophic Times: Resisting the Coming Barbarism*, 62.

Practising how to pay attention carries the radical possibility to notice what we have been expected to ignore. It is hard to navigate all that is calling our attention in this world. Perception theory shows us that we need to shut off a lot of noise to make sense of what we hear, to register what is important, and manage it to our comprehension. Inability to do so makes us overstimulated, overloaded, unable to systematize and comprehend. Through our lives we have learned how to systematize and direct our focus, and we continually practice how to direct our attention.

The guided meditations invite the participants to practice shifting their attention, starting from the visual input that dominates the days for most of us, to favour listening, smelling, tasting, touching and allowing ourselves to remember and imagine. This practice engages learning with all the senses. By bringing awareness to our sense of smell, taste and touch, as well as to the audible world around us, attention is shifted from habitually prioritizing the visual above other senses.

Learning in an embodied way, makes it possible to make use of all the data we receive through our senses. This favors understandings that might be beyond words and language, that are felt and sensed. Making intelligible the range of ways we experience ourselves in the world, offers a fuller, more complex view. It offers an experience of the subject we are studying.

Meditation can also activate the memories that the body holds, to open up pathways or make connections, where connection might have been lost. Sometimes that means trying to bring attention to things that might need to be unlearned, parts that have hardened, that need softening up to change. These memories can better our understanding of a subject, rooting what we learn in our own experience.

Meditation is not intended as an escape from the present, but as a shift in attention from what occupies our minds in the busy everyday, to how the present moment impacts our body-minds. Many of the suggestions I use are intended to have the participant imbued with the present, to make them hyper attentive to the now. Instead of starting sentences with "imagine that you..." the language is more direct, proposing that you are *always already in it*. You are always already breathing, resting in this chair or on this floor, in this space. You are always already connected to the world and the people around you. You are always already in the presence of knowledge and you are always already studying.[93]

The practice of meditation offers training for readiness through focused attention. Being hyper attentive to what is going on with us helps us to be able to deal with uncertainty. Practising attentiveness is a way to improve our perception of, and sensitivity to, others and the world. It brings us in closer awareness of how we are connected to the world around us, and how this impacts us. In recognizing where we are, we can find our bearings in the midst of uncertainty. It might offer a state of readiness for an unknown that surprises.

The role of the guide and the teacher

I have two roles that differ, but that are also similar: the performance artist leading the audience in participatory performance, and the teacher in different art school classrooms. In this project I explore both, and in my practice they sometimes overlap: I lecture in art spaces and perform in classrooms.

For pedagogy attention is central. When we shift our attention to a subject, it activates our relationship to it. This is one of the robust meanings of study – to pay a subject our attention. In teaching, a lot of effort is put into keeping and directing the attention of students. In performance, we have a similar relationship to the audience. This requires of us, as teachers and performers, to be truly present.

It has become more and more apparent to me how my state of mind, and how it reflects in my body, sets a tone for the class. It has brought me to think about how I enter; how I greet people, how I move in the space, the tempo of my movements – even my breathing. How and when I call the class to order, and how I address them when I do. Sometimes I manage to ease the transition between what is already happening and what we are about to do, so that no call to order is needed. With time, it is possible to work towards a setting

93 Harney and Moten, *The Undercommons*.

where the work has already started before I enter, and continues when I leave.

Teaching is also about paying attention. To hold the space of the classroom takes a lot of energy (my armpits are usually sweaty after teaching). We pay attention to what is happening in the room, to how people respond to the material that is presented to them, and how they respond to us and each other. We navigate distractions from the outside, conflicts that arise, insecurities that need to be addressed, miscommunication, group dynamics, and peoples physical and psychological needs. When I teach, I come with a framework and a set of exercises and tasks, but the order usually changes as we go along. In my head, there are endless recalculations going on; like a GPS when you take the wrong turn, I need to find other paths when the group reacts to what is put forth.

In my role as the teacher, I do not have a clear progression or end goal with my teaching any more. When I started teaching I made my plans minute-by-minute, one thing leading up to the next, withholding information when needed to get the right twists and turns, and a finale at the end. The dramaturgy was strong in order to keep the attention of the students. The aim of the workshops was clearly stated, to myself and to the students, and was often concluded in the production of something tangible that would mark the end of the workshop.

Growing more confident in my teaching, I have learned that I need to let go of control. My focus has shifted to practice being present, and to pay more attention to how to adapt to the room and the people in it. I still come ambitiously prepared, but primarily with a place to start and a box full of pedagogical tools. I still have things I would like to come across; data to present, a theory or hypothesis, questions I want to bring attention to, things I would like to remind the students of with the help of hints, questions and maybes. But I let the direction of the progression and the tempo of the teaching adapt to the people in the room and the conditions for us coming together. I expect my plans to change with the group, and I hope that we will end up in unexpected places.

I know the aim of my teaching in terms of my intent, rather than my goal. I come to study, together with the students. To teach that which I most need to learn[94], on the edge of what I know. I come with curiosity for the subject as well as for the students and the place we are in.

When constructing the guided meditations, I start out with researching the place and context of the invitation, learning about the place and the people who will be there. I find points of connection and interests, and formulate a subject or intention to guide my writing. Often, the guided meditations are site specific (the Museum Quarters in Vienna for *Enter/Exit*, the Academy building at Schillerplatz for *Unsettling I* and the city of Venice for *Unsettling II)*, other times it is the subject matter that forms the space (the shape shifting body in *FEELERS*).

Before I can take the role of the guide, I have to make the journey myself. I start a process of listening and speaking to the place and to the subject that the guided meditation is trying to address. I pay attention to the space, I study it, I meditate on it and wait for what will come to mind. I close my eyes. I shift attention through the body to see what parts respond to the place. I will have to take this journey several times to see where it leads me.

I write down notes, words and sentences, falling into a rhythm of speaking that keeps the momentum of the moment. The text is performative from the start; it is a manuscript with chapters and pauses. In rehearsal, the performative element is elaborated on, experimenting with changing the rhythm, where to put emphasis, where to breathe, striving to find rhythm and tone. The aim is to find a balance between the momentum and the need for breaks and pauses.

Later on in the process I add sound. I have gone from using prefabricated sound, via my own sound experiments, to collaborating with sound artist Julia Giertz[95]. Giertz comes from a background as a dancer and have investigated sound as touch for several years. We came together in a mutual interest for how bodies are affected by words, waves and vibrations. The introduction of sound has allowed

94 Alexander, *Pedagogies of Crossing: Meditations on Feminism, Sexual Politics, Memory and the Sacred*, 22.

95 Find out more about Julia Giertz work at https://juliagiertz.info/

for more complex parameters to account for; the space sound makes, how vibrations trigger the body's organs, and the feelings, thoughts and memories that arise from that. The collaboration with Julia has been fundamental in adding a whole other dimension to the guided meditations. It is all her making, and I have totally trusted her expertise.[96]

Recording my voice has given me the opportunity to dive more into vocal work. I have become better at articulating and projecting into the room, making sure that each word comes across. Recording has confirmed the importance of practicing being present, so that the meaning and emotional attachment to the words comes through, allowing emotions to affect my vocal cords. We chose not to clean up the sound too much or edit out the sound of my breathing, to keep a sense of intimacy. In the process of recording, the repetition of takes works as an editing process as well, firming up the text and cutting out redundant bits.

Participation starts with an invitation. In neither performance nor teaching participation can be taken for granted. There is an agreement between teacher and student, performer and audience, guide and participant, that needs to be articulated, negotiated and honored. As with any relationship there needs to be a mutual trust, which demands an element of risk-taking. – *I invite you to take this journey with me. – I trust you and will follow your lead.*

All my meditations come with instructions for how to prepare. The instructions have developed over time, to clear up misconceptions and make sure that participation comes with the proper information. They contain information about the length of the meditation, what to do with your shoes and jacket, where to start. I give you the options of lying down or sitting up, informing that sitting up usually gives you a bit more agency, and if you are tired, lying down can have you fall asleep. I assure that it is OK to drift in and out of the moment. I also like to inform of possible triggers; even though covering all the possible things that could cause upset is not possible, I

96 There has not been room for a chapter on sound in this dissertation, but I hope we get a chance to write it together at some point.

find that including some of the things that seem to repeatedly trigger people, helps with reminding participants that there might be content that you are not ready for today. Most important is the reminder that you can stop at any time, and giving you some options; to open your eyes, change position, take off your headphones or leave the room.

In the classroom the guided meditations are integrated in the teaching. I have often offered meditations as an introduction to a subject; a time travel back to a few months ago, to investigate the experience of entering the art academy; a journey to the bottom of the sea, to investigate our relationship to the big blue; a journey into a body that shape shifts, to investigate our embodied memories.

The invitation can come as a surprise to the students, as this format is not very common in the visual arts school classroom. The biggest hurdle to overcome is usually to involve the body in such an explicit way. To have students put down their pen and computer, take off their shoes, leave their desk and sit on the floor and to close their eyes. It is a break in the teaching format and in the way bodies are usually carried in the classroom. I always make sure to express that participation is voluntary, but I recognize that there is an inherent pressure to partake.

Art spaces are usually less contained; doors opening, people passing through, it is easier to leave. The agreement is temporary and the roles are not as fixed. Generally, I have to put in more effort for people to accept the invitation to participate. The audience comes to experience something, but are usually also in a critical mode (What is this? Why are we doing this? Who are you?) and a social mode (Who else is here? How are the others reacting?). A critical mass usually helps, like friends in the audience.

I usually use transparency and context to establish trust. I give an introduction to the work, some context to how it came to be, and present the time limit. I offer exit strategies; that you can open your eyes at any time, and you can leave without being confronted with questions. I warn that this can be an unsettling experience. The use of "guided meditation", as a self-explanatory title, sets the expectation of what is going to happen. Many people I encounter in these rooms have some experience in somatic group activities like yoga, dance, martial arts or gym classes, so they are used to being led in this way.

I use my voice and body language to build trust and set the mode. I try to have a calm and steady voice, slow breathing, no rush (though nervousness sometimes gets in the way). Eyes steady, jaws relaxed, wrists bare and open. I move slower than usual and try not to rush people. With a slight turn away from the audience, I make clear that I will not watch them, not judge them, in how they choose to participate. This is important. Giving the audience or students a moment to choose where and how they want to sit, is a way to open up a path to participation. This works as a suggestion – when you have made the easy choice of where to sit, you have also, unconsciously, made the harder choice of participation. You have accepted the invitation.

Resistance

To counteract the persuasiveness of the guided meditations, I have built in space for resistance, mainly by adding breaks in the trajectory of the meditations. It is easy for the participant, once they have started to say yes to my invitations, to get caught up in the momentum and keep saying yes, without real agency. To counteract this logic, I have tried to introduce moments in the meditations, obstructions or breaks, where you are snapped out of the trajectory of the story, and have a chance to reject the invitation to continue.

In *Enter/Exit – A mediation to the point of no return* this happens in the moments of self-reflection, when the protagonist think about their clothes and how they do, or do not, fit in. It is kind of a funny moment, and a reminder of the insecurities that can come with the situation that you are in and the people you are with. It has a different tone than the rest of the story. In the meditation *Unsettling II: A guided meditation to the sea*, the obstruction comes when it is time to adapt to the sea and start breathing water. The voice describes what is coming up, and that it will be uncomfortable, making a break before the journey continues. The sound also changes in both tempo and intensity, changing from slow, seductive sounds to rhythmic layers that speed up the heart rate. The voice introduces agency by suggesting that you have to be active in this process, and do the hard work of learning to breath differently. These breaks offer a moment for self-recognition, a chance to step out of oneself to look at what is happening, and reflect on whether to proceed.

In the classroom, I try to find ways to welcome resistance to my teaching. This is not a comfortable practice. Being questioned is unsettling, and can be both triggering and exhausting. It often comes in the form of passive expressions, since questioning the authority of the teacher is not an easy move to make. This means we also have to pay attention to the signs of resistance, and what they want to express, remembering that resistance comes with a story.

It is up to us as teachers to interpret the behaviours of our students from a standpoint of them being complete human beings and full worthy subjects. Their reasons for being here might differ from what we expect. The knowledge they bring might be beyond our scope. Taking seriously the equality of intelligence[97] and the importance of difference, means we will have to make this effort, however imperfect. Carving out the space needed for resistance to be expressed, is also a way to teach that resistance is possible, that it is worth the uncomfortable effort, and this knowledge will allow them to resist in other important settings.[98]

When moments of resistance are expressed clearly, it usually causes an interruption, that makes us hesitate, and re-think, maybe take a few steps back and analyze what we have done so far. It is a sweaty moment for the teacher, I will not lie. But it is exciting as well, as it is bound to disrupt the hierarchy of the classroom. It says something about trust, as our ability to handle the questions that are put to us comes to the test. This is when practicing paying attention, as a teacher, is put into play.

Carving out space for resistance in the classroom takes a similar form as in the guided meditation. Adding moments of disruption, where we step out of the flow of what we are working on, to reflect

---

97 Jacques Rancière, *The Ignorant Schoolmaster, Five Lessons in Intellectual Emancipation* (Stanford, California: Stanford University Press, 1991), 45.

98 Recommended reading: Jay Gillen, Educating for Insurgency: The Roles of Young People in Schools of Poverty (Oakland: AK Press, 2014).

on what we have done so far and where we are heading, offering a moment to give input on how to best continue. Taking feedback repeatedly through the course. Arranging for students to have conversations without the teacher present, and time for themselves to gather their thoughts. Returning reminders that participation is voluntary, and can take different forms.

Sometimes, it is just about allowing resistance to be, without trying to persuade or convince the student to let down their guard, trusting that they have their reasons.

Shifting the role of the guide

Apart from the guided meditations that I have presented as a lecture or as a performance, I have made two sound installation for art spaces, one in Venice for the Biennial in 2017 and one in Malmö for the sound festival INTONAL. This entails not being in the room when the participants experience them. I do not generally do art works that travel without me, so for me, this is largely uncharted territory. I prefer to be in the room with the audience and I have developed an artistic practice to accommodate that, but in these cases I went out of my comfort zone and adapted to how the contemporary art world generally prefer to operate; with delimited art objects that can be presented in a white cube or black box.

Not being able to witness the audience's response, nor being able to adapt or respond, has made me question what is possible within this format. If something goes wrong, I am not there to care for you. It lacks in response-ability – the ability to properly care and respond, and in accountability for what is put out there[99]. The general feedback on the work has been rather positive, but I still fear that the installation format does not sufficiently hold the space that is needed for this practice. Can people fully engage with the work in an exhibition setting? Can they find the focus to switch their attention from other artworks, audience members etc.? Is the in-person contact with me as a guide necessary to offer the trust that is needed?

99 Donna Haraway, *Staying with the Trouble: Making Kin in the Chthulucene* (Durham and London: Duke University Press, 2016), 105.

The experienced art audience are probably capable of directing their focus, feeling safe and comfortable in this setting. But if you are not? Am I over- or underestimating my audience? Maybe this is primarily my experience, that I just *do not like it*; the one-way direction of the work, and the distance that is put between me and the audience. Maybe I just prefer to do it differently.

Working with installation prompted a question in Julia Giertz and me about accessibility. We decided to publish a sound piece online for headphones, in Swedish this time, and at our own initiative. We wanted to respond to the rise of fascism we could see around us, and to think about how to handle this frightening reality collectively, resulting in the piece *Anti-fascistisk gatumeditation* (Anti-fascist street meditation) published on May 1st 2019. Publishing online was an opportunity to actively find an audience outside the contemporary art world, reaching out to our activist friends and family. The aim was utilitarian; the guided meditation is intended for a daily commute or evening walk, to be used repeatedly when necessary. The audio was mixed to work on a range of headphones and the piece could be streamed or downloaded to a phone or other device. We supplemented the online publishing by arranging collective walks with the meditation playing individually in everyone's headphones, for a shared experience. When, a year later, Covid-19 struck and made gathering for demonstrations impossible, the online guided meditation gained new momentum as an alternative to gathering physically.

In the case of online publishing, my experience from this example is that the increased accessibility triumphs the need for an in-person meeting. More of agency is left to the participants, who can choose when and where to listen, on what device and at what volume. They can encounter the work in a familiar setting, without some of the high thresholds that frame the contemporary art scene. Not to claim that online publishing automatically reaches anyone, it has its own limitations both in terms of technical access and online algorithms, but it is possible to instigate a sort of sharing by word of mouth that organically spreads and reaches a different audience than the art spaces can. Encountering the work via a recommendation from someone you know establishes another form of trust of a more collective nature.

Seemingly contradictory, the loss of control for me as the artist and guide feels like a step in the right direction. Not losing control to the institution, as with the installation practice, but losing control to the participant, by allowing the work to enter the participant's private sphere. It offers a more intimate setting for the work, to hear the guided meditation one ones own headphones, in ones own living room or neighbourhood. In a pedagogical sense, it offers the possibility to hand over the practice of study to the participant, rather than to hold on too tightly to teaching.

As part of this project, I have experimented with workshops where the participants have practised to construct and share guided meditations with each other. This has mainly been done in art spaces, in workshops directed to artists. In the workshops, I have asked the group to define some common theme or subject that they want to approach. For instance, at Milvus Artistic Research Center we researched the old story of a big sheatfish that was supposed to have lived in the stream just outside our windows. At Tjörnedala Konsthall, as well as at the Press to Exit Project Space in Skopje, we looked into different iterations of the future of visual art. Divided into groups, the participants then wrote collective texts that were turned into short guided meditations. We discussed how to formulate suggestions, how to lead people in and out of the meditation, the use of voice, rhythm, sound etc. In the end, we got to experience the guided meditations that each group had created, and shared a moment to evaluate the experience.

My main take away from these workshops is how the construction and experience of guided meditations can function as a creative practice. The feedback I got from participants was that constructing guided meditations could be used as a research method in their artistic practice, as a way to approach a new subject with all senses activated. It could widen the experience of a subject, from gathering data and analysing it, to trying to actually *feel* the subject. It helped with shifting perspective, to imagine oneself in the body of a subject, or in another space and time.

The guided meditations presented in these short workshops were surprisingly effective. People seemed to shift between roles with ease, trusting each other to lead and to be led. For me, it has been an opportunity to pass on the experiment with guided meditation to other artists, and watch what they can do with it. I would love for this to play a bigger part in artistic research, to find ways to pass on our methods and findings to other artists.

III: INTERRUPTING THE LINEARITY OF CRITICAL CONCIOUSNESS THEORY

This chapter starts out rather condensed, in an attempt to establish the main concepts and characters, before it opens up with questions, stories and examples. I recommend you to take your time; read slowly, breath slowly, and trust that the tempo will pick up the further we get into it. Investigating the different facets of our consciousness is no casual quest and no breezy business. But we will practice how to stay and play in this double bind.

An introduction to critical consciousness

The concept of critical consciousness is present in different strands of radical and critical pedagogy[100]. Though contested regularly[101], it seems to re-emerge again and again. Critical consciousness is a central element of the empowering process; making the student conscious of their situation, aware of themselves and the systems that govern their lives, and from that awareness become willing and able to act towards change. It stands as the confirmation that the student is empowered with agency to change the world.

The aim of raising consciousness as an element of pedagogy is not only epistemological, it is ontological – it suggests another way of being in the world. It suggests transformation of self, a shift in disposition, a way of becoming. It suggests not only knowing more, in an additive sense of learning, but of becoming different, by attaining another level of consciousness. Acquiring an awareness of the world and of self, and of how they are connected.

It points to the fact that we teach something other than the contents of our subjects. Things happen in education that are beyond the mere transference of knowledge, and our pedagogical efforts contain an inclination to support people in becoming, in transformation. This becoming is not inherently good. On the contrary, as teachers, we have a tendency to steer students in the direction of assimilation – of becoming *better* students, *better* citizens, *better* artists – where *better* is in line with what we once have been taught, or with adapting to the status quo.

But even when we do not; when we consciously direct the students towards being dissidents to power and becoming agents of change – what does that make us as teachers? What manipulation or coercion do we allow ourselves in the service of radical change?

---

100 In the field of critical pedagogy it is used by, among others, Henry Giroux and Peter McLaren. In radical pedagogy I include feminist pedagogy as well as postcolonial, decolonial and indigenous pedagogy, see for example bell hooks, Gayatri Chakravorty Spivak, Chandra Talpade Mohanty and M. Jacqui Alexander.

101 See for example Peter Berger's critique in *Pyramids of Sacrifice: Political Ethics and Social Change* from 1974, or more recently Tuck and Yang, *Decolonization Is Not a Metaphor* from 2012

What does it say about us and about our relationship to the students?

M. Jacqui Alexander, Afro-Caribbean writer and professor of Gender Studies in Toronto, writes:

> I have not always been successful in simply teaching in order to teach, to teach that which I most needed to learn. More often I intended my teaching to serve as a conduit to radicalization, which I now understand to mean a certain imprisonment that conflates the terms of domination with the essence of life. Similar to the ways in which domination always already confounds our sex with all of who we are, the focus on radicalization always already turns our attention to domination. The point is not to supplant a radical curriculum. The question is whether we can simply teach in order to teach.[102]

MY WISH FOR A RADICAL PEDAGOGY has gone through a shift, similar to what M. Jaqui Alexander unfolds in this quote. It is a shift from a pedagogy in the service of creating political subjects (what Alexander refers to as radicalization), to what I would consider a much more disobedient and subversive position, where the radical shift lies in unsettling my position as teacher; teaching what I most need to learn, developing a trust in the surprises my students will bring and foster in myself a radical openness to change that is beyond what I can imagine. A shift towards the unknown. This demands a level of self-actualization or hyper-self-reflexivity articulated in the writings of bell hooks and Gayatri Chakravorty Spivak.

A shift towards the unknown opens up towards more than the teacher can imagine, to what is beyond our horizon, beyond our knowing. It acknowledges the limits of our knowledge, the partial-

---

102 Alexander, *Pedagogies of Crossing: Meditations on Feminism, Sexual Politics, Memory and the Sacred*, 23.

ity of it, and the need to put trust in a pedagogy that supposes an equality of intelligence with the students[103]. It puts focus on our ability to hold the classroom we create in suspension.

A shift towards the unknown must not, however, be used as an excuse to opt out of the ethical and the political. We still work towards change, and that change cannot take any direction. If we aim towards a more just world, we will have to carry the responsibility of directing our efforts accordingly. A pedagogy of radical openness does not come with a goal, but with intention. Here, I turn to Gayatri Chakravorty Spivak for help. With the figure of the double bind we are reminded that, while there is no closing the ethical gap, we still have to strive to supplement it. We will not leave the historical or ethical behind. Even though we cannot disclose a plan (or curriculum) for how change will happen, we can still show places where to start. We can offer work to do.

Examining the concept of "critical consciousness" as a foundation of how we think and do radical pedagogy, is part of doing Spivak's homework[104]. It is part of examining the foundations of our believes and our complicity in systems of oppression. Paulo Freire's writing has been indispensable to me in my search for a radical pedagogy, and his work continue to show up in writings and conversations about radical and critical education to this day. That is why it felt important for me to go to the source and find my own interpretation of his work.

His works on critical consciousness are vague in the sense that he offers no manual, no techniques, but are generous with ideas that are supplemented with a few concrete examples from his teaching. This leaves his work open to interpretation. My interest is not so much in how this plays out in the individual (as in individual development theory for example), but in the potential for collective, political change. For this we must read him in his specific historical and political context. At the same time, I want to be able to implement these ideas in the classroom. Freire's work is sometimes contradictory in

---

103 Rancière, *The Ignorant Schoolmaster, Five Lessons in Intellectual Emancipation*, 45.

104 Gayatri Chakravorty Spivak, *The Post-Colonial Critic: Interviews, Strategies, Dialogues* (New York, NY: Routledge, 1990), 62.

terms of the relationship between teacher and students – who becomes conscious, and of what? What happens in this linear telling – what was before consciousness? What is the teacher's role in doing the "awakening"?

I will try to untangle some of these ideas and questions in this chapter. Mainly by tracing the teachings of Paulo Freire, displacing the concepts of naïve and magic consciousness, and contrasting his line of thought with that of Gloria Anzaldúa and W.E.B. Du Bois. It is partly a critique of Freire's writing, but I am not disregarding critical consciousness as a concept as much as supplementing it (with the naïve and the magical) and unsettling it (with the oppositional stance of double and mestiza consciousness). To elaborate on how this could translate to the classroom, I will offer examples from my own teaching as well as from my experiments with guided meditations as a pedagogical and performative practice. The questions in this text stem from a recognition that what we as radical teachers have done has not been enough – what I have done has not been enough – to stay true to the change we want to see in the world.

The role of the teacher in Paulo Freire's pedagogy

Fundamental for current ideas of critical consciousness in education is Paulo Freire's *conscientização* (in Portuguese), referred to as *conscientization* in English. This describes the process of an individual or a community to uncover, reflect and act on the root causes for their oppression, and in this process overcoming the alienation that stands in the way of freedom. An individual going through this process is referred to as developing *a critical consciousness*.[105]

The oppressed106, in Freire's telling, are confined to inaction by the way the oppressors have infiltrated their consciousness. The education provided by the oppressors are set in place to teach the oppressed to accept and adapt to a situation where they are deemed inferior, lazy and incompetent. This is implemented through what

105 Freire, *Pedagogy of the Oppressed*.

106 Freire uses the division oppressed and oppressor as the main characters in his book. They are inextricably linked by the conditions of oppression, and despite being on the opposite sides of oppression, it strips them both of their humanity.

is referred to as "the banking system", where the teacher deposits knowledge in the students as if they were a bank[107]. The students arrive to the classroom as empty vessels. There is no mutual exchange or room for reflection.

The goal of Paulo Freire's liberatory project is for all men and women to be "more fully human"[108]. He views oppression mainly as a question of alienation, rather than of one group being dominant over the other. The task of uprooting the system of oppression is put on the oppressed, and in the process of their liberation their oppressors will also be freed. The educator, placed on the side of the oppressor, cannot liberate the oppressed, they can only make it their mission to stand with the oppressed and fight by their side for freedom[109]. The teacher will support his students in their emancipation, and in the awakening of a critical consciousness (for the good of all humankind).

In Freire's writing, the practice of critique is not only presented as an analytical skill or a set of methods, but as a state of mind – a critical consciousness. In order to reach our full humanity, we have to attain this other level of awareness. This is achieved by the uncovering of the mechanics of systematic oppression, combined with a practice of self-reflection. The systematic oppression can be deemed manageable by defining its part as "limit-situations"[110]. Limit-situations are the concrete situations where we experience the limitations that oppression puts on us. With the historically bound and situated knowledge of our situation, we do not regard the limit-situations as fetters that bounds us, but as obstacles that can be overcome. It reveals the border between us as is, and us as more fullyw human, and this revelation activates us. It is in the combination of action and reflection (in praxis) that the power of *conscientization* comes true.

Critical consciousness is also defined by its negation. It differen-

107 Freire, *Pedagogy of the Oppressed*, 72.

108 Freire, 44. "Men and women" are the terms used by Freire to supposedly cover all adult humans. The emphasis of humanity as the goal of our strivings can be read both in the light of the human rights movement at the time, and in the Christian humanist tradition that Freire was part of.

109 Freire, 39.

110 Freire, 99.

tiates from what Freire calls *naïve* and *magic consciousness*. He projects that these are the levels of consciousness inhabited by most illiterates he meets in his teaching. With a naïve consciousness, you see the world as static and consider yourself superior to facts, and free to understand them in any way that pleases you. With a magic consciousness you assign all facts to a higher power, out of your control, and this renders you passive. In neither of these you have the ability to analyse your situation, and cannot identify the actions to overcome it.[111]

> "The more accurately men grasp true causality, the more critical their understanding of reality will be. Their understanding will be magical to the degree that they fail to grasp causality. Further, critical consciousness always submits that causality to analysis; what is true today may not be so tomorrow. Naïve consciousness sees causality as a static, established fact, and thus is deceived in its perception.
> Critical consciousness represents 'things and facts as they exist empirically in their cultural and circumstantial correlations... naïve consciousness considers itself superior to facts, in control of facts and thus free to understand them as it pleases'.[112]

MAGIC CONSCIOUSNESS, IN CONTRAST, simply apprehends facts and attributes to them a superior power by which it is controlled and to which it must therefore submit. Magic consciousness is characterized by fatalism which leads man to fold their arms, resigned to the impossibility of resisting the power of facts.

Critical consciousness is integrated with reality; naïve consciousness superimposes itself on reality; and fanatical consciousness, whose pathological naïveté leads to irrational, adapts to reality."

Freire displays a disproportionate trust in rationality, truth and

111 Freire, *Education for Critical Consciousness*, 39.
112 Freire, 39.

accuracy, as the catalyst that will lead to action. According to Freire, critical consciousness is integrated in reality in a way that naïve and magic consciousness are not. When the student apprehends a phenomenon or a problem, they also apprehend its causal links. Critical consciousness always submits this causality to analysis. The more accurately the student apprehend what Freire considers "true causality", the more critical their analysis will be. The aim is for a critical understanding to lead to critical action, in contrast to naïve or magical thinking that only leads to passive fatalism.[113]

What is the role of the teacher in the process of *conscientization*? The teacher supports the students in an "awakening" of their consciousness[114]. Their task is to help the student to overcome their tendencies towards naïve or magical thinking, to "discover themselves". This is done through dialogue, in which the teacher is helping students to break down and decode the world around them.

Dialogue is at the centre of Freire's pedagogical theory. This is the mode of transaction that replaces the banking method. Dialogue is based on the word as praxis – the combination of action and reflection.[115] A "true word" is bound by praxis – when uttered it transforms the world. By naming the world we make our claim to understand it as well as to create it. In dialogue, the oppressed attain an attitude of creation and re-creation – an ability to intervene in their own context, in a process of transforming the world as well as themselves.

According to Freire, dialogue comes out of a horizontal relationship. Dialogue demands humility – you cannot be in dialogue from a place of arrogance. Humility requires that you consider yourself as mortal as every other human, as well as recognizing your dependency on others. We are all trying to understand the world, and transform it, by taking part in the naming of the world. Dialogue

113 Freire, 39–40.

114 Freire, 38.

115 Freire locates action and reflections as the elementary components of the word. "Lacking in one, the other inevitably suffers: action without reflections amounts to mere activism, action for action's own sake, while reflection without action amounts to verbalism, (...) into an alienated and alienating 'blah.'". *Freire, Pedagogy of the Oppressed,* 68.

also demands a faith in human kind, a faith in people, and must come from a place of love, from a commitment to others. Built on this foundation of humility, faith and love, dialogue becomes a horizontal relationship based on mutual trust, Freire argues.116

Freire proposes that the horizontal relationship of radical education undoes the teacher-student relation, in favour of "teacher-student with students-teachers"[117]. In this situation both are subjects in their own right, and learning happens in both directions. The teacher joins the students in a shared endeavour of fellow inquiry. They break out of their respective roles to become authentic human beings, together.

A contradiction in the pedagogy of emancipation

How does the idea of a horizontal relationship between teacher-student and student-teacher coincide with the teacher's role in an awakening of critical consciousness?

To be freed, the oppressed need to uncover how power influences their repressed consciousness. But, to be able to do that, someone whose consciousness is *not* under the influence of power needs to reveal those powers structures to them. Gert Biesta, Dutch professor in Public Education, has identified a contradiction built into what he calls "the modern logic of emancipation"[118]. It is the idea that someone from the outside sits on the information needed to free the oppressed. The teacher enters, already knowing objective truths about the life and world of the students (the one's who are to be emancipated), and by revealing those truths the students can enter the world of the teacher and become their equal. There is dependency built into this system, where the oppressed do not possess what is needed to free themselves. They need someone from the outside – a teacher – to give them the right information.

According to Biesta, Freire does not subscribe to this logic. By undoing the role of the teacher as authority, Freire takes the teacher

116 Freire, *Pedagogy of the Oppressed*, 89–93.
117 Freire, 80.
118 Gert Biesta, "Don't Be Fooled by Ignorant Schoolmasters: On the Role of the Teacher in Emancipatory Education," *Policy Futures in Education* 15, no. 1 (January 1, 2017): 62.

out of the equation, leaving a classroom of equals. Still, there is a clear linearity in how he describes the awakening of the student's consciousness that contradicts this claim to equality. There is a before and after; before you were naïve, now you are critical; before you were asleep, now you are awake. There is a fundamental linear idea of emancipation, where the teacher is lifting the student out of ignorance, up to his level of consciousness. From this new position they can meet as equals, as teacher-students and student-teachers, and join in fellow investigations, and creative acts of naming and transforming the world.

For Freire the classroom is a place of coming together, of unity. There is recognition of the difference, power relations and hierarchies between the oppressors and the oppressed in the outer world, but the classroom is staged as a place where this power relation is undone. He does not address the difference between individual students, how they relate to each other, or various levels of experience and capacity to engage.

In Freire's writing, he tends to speak in the voice of a teacher who knows the truth about the world, about authenticity, about what is a "true" word, and what is "true" reflection. This claim to truth and authenticity signals that the teacher is in a position of knowledge that highly differs from that of the student. This authoritative voice reinforces the contradiction between the teacher as authority and the teacher as a teacher-student.

A possible key to understanding the contradictory roles of the teacher can be found in Biesta's proposal that there are two different stages in Freire's pedagogy119. In the examples of teaching situations in both *Pedagogy of the Oppressed* and *Teaching for Critical Consciousness* the teacher does not join on equal terms with the students: they enter at a stage *before* liberation. What stands in the way of liberation is the oppressed consciousness. "Submerged in this reality, the oppressed cannot perceive clearly the 'order' which serves the interests of the oppressors whose image they have internalized."[120]

---

119 Biesta, 65.
120 Freire, *Pedagogy of the Oppressed*, 62.

Being totally submerged in an oppressed consciousness, the oppressed cannot start to perceive themselves as subjects of their own lives. They also do not have the political power to change their situation. So the teacher, on the side of the oppressed, inserts himself to prompt the start of the revolution. Freire places the teacher as part of a "revolutionary leadership"[121]. In his role as a leader, the teacher cannot simply copy the pedagogy of the oppressors, using the banking method to push a revolutionary agenda. Instead, the leadership must work co-intentionally with the oppressed, through dialogue, and in a process of mutual becoming.

This suggestion of the two steps in Freire's pedagogy could clarify some of the contradictions in his writing, but somehow the larger contradiction remains: if the awakening of a critical consciousness demands dialogue, and true dialogue demands a horizontal relationship, then where is this pedagogical process of emancipation supposed to begin? Where do we start?

Freire believed that the content of education must be found in people's reality and in their perception of the world. In *Teaching for Critical Consciousness*, Freire presents examples from a project where he and his colleagues were teaching people in rural Brazil to read and write. By spending time in the countryside and with the people, they were able to find the *general themes* of the education[122], and to draw them out in a series of *situations*: scenes from everyday life that became the basis of the lessons. These are documented in the book as a series of illustrations.

The illustrations picture everyday situations, like a hunter hunting, and objects, like a vase with flowers. Others are more staged with symbolism, like that of a man in a field with a tool in one hand

---

121 Freire, 67.

122 Freire asks that we locate the meaningful thematics of the people, what he calls *generative themes*. Every epoch in history is constituted by a collection of ideas, concepts, hopes, doubts, values and challenges, and the concrete representation of these, including their opposites or obstacles, constitutes the peoples themes of that epoch. As examples Freire names *domination*, and its opposite *liberation*, to be themes of his times. When confronted with the general themes, people respond differently; some work to uphold the structures, others to change them. Every theme contains obstacles, or limit-situations, that should be presented in the classroom as challenges that demands a response, not just verbally but in terms of action.

and a book in the other. Each illustration is accompanied by a description of how the dialogue with the students developed. These descriptions neatly follow the progression of critical consciousness described by Freire in the first part of the book.

When looking at these illustrations, it is not obvious for me how the situations started the discussions that follow. The conversations described are elaborate reflections on nature vs culture, on how culture comes to be, on history and democracy. I am not questioning that these conversations took place; what I am wondering is how they were prompted.

For example, there is a strong emphasis on the man as subject and centre of the illustrations. There is a logic to that choice, since it was the men of the population that they were teaching, but it also reflects how they perceived the population, or at least how they expected the men they were teaching to perceive it. We cannot know how much was legitimately researched, and how much was projection. At least, I do not have the situational knowledge to unpack that.

To me, it seems that these illustrations are projections of the teachers' wishes for their students. The topics of discussion come first, the situations enter to support the topic, and the questions asked by the teacher follow a predetermined idea of progression. It is indeed important to ground the topics of discussion in the lived reality of the students, and that effort is definitely there. But to claim this as a situation of co-intention, and even co-creation, I believe is an overstatement.

What I read is the teachers coming with the intention of persuading their students of the importance of literacy, the importance of the word, and the word as a means for transformation and freedom. Freedom as in democracy, and in humanity. These are amiable goals, but they are predetermined, and formulated in a Western canon of human rights and Western modelled democracy as the model of freedom. The path for emancipation is set. Can we think of other models that do not predetermine the path of emancipation? Can we imagine another route for this pedagogy?

The contribution of Freire's project is undeniable. Even considering the lives and experiences of his students, the illiterate population of Brazil, was a radical move, and continues to be so in many cases123. Still, I am lacking a reflection from Freire on how this consideration manifested, how the process unfolded, and the role of the teachers in it. What made them so certain that they could decipher the situation of the lives they were not a part of?

The contradiction at the core of the modern logic of emancipation becomes clear: the relation to truth is evident to the teacher, but not to the student. There is little call for reflection on through what lens the teacher perceives the reality of the student, or how the teacher interprets their reality of the student to fit into what he believes to be the truth. What is the truth that the teacher brings? And how does the teacher verify what is true?

That leads me to the second question: what if what the teachers would consider naïve or magical thinking, could actually have some value? What if they recognized what they discarded as knowledge to be cared for and learned from?

Thirdly: what would happen if the teachers could imagine challenging their own assumptions, and open up to the naïve or magical thinking they themselves might be prone to? The things we take for granted, our core beliefs and values, our unfounded assumptions, our unreasonable fantasies. If we recognize these negative aspects of naïve and magic consciousness, they should also be accounted for.

The idea of a critical consciousness is widely used in both the academic field of critical pedagogy, in feminist and decolonial pedagogy, as well as in activism. We obviously crave and need it. But maybe there is cause to be more precise in how we use this term that Freire coined, and of our intentions for using it? The language of *Pedagogy of the Oppressed* is situated in its own time and place. Freire's humanist and Christian background clearly influenced how he developed his pedagogical projects, as well as the human rights based activism in the Global South and the early formulation of the

123 As an example, look to the appendix "Konstverkstad"; and I would like to recommend Jay Gillen "Teaching for Insurgency: the roles of young people in schools of poverty".

post-colonial project. His use of human and humanity can be more thoroughly addressed, as well as the sometimes rigid division of oppressors and oppressed.[124]

So how can we use our intersectional feminist, decolonial and queer knowledges to address his work, with its contradictions and gaps? What do we need to be able to situate these pedagogical offerings to another time and place?

To unsettle the role of the teacher

Elisabeth Ellsworth, American professor of Media Studies, makes an early attempt at addressing the field of critical pedagogy in her text "Why Doesn't This Feel Empowering? Working Through the Repressive Myths of Critical Pedagogy"[125] from 1988. At that time the field was just establishing, led by authors like Henry Giroux and Peter McLaren, mainly white male academics, who built their theories heavily on Freire. Ellsworth, initially positive to critical pedagogy as a concept and using it in descriptions of her own courses, expresses her frustration when trying to implement some of these ideas in her teaching. She comes to realize that many of the key concepts of critical pedagogy, as *dialogue*, *student voice* and *empowerment* actually work as repressive. Her critique comes from a feminist standpoint, and an intersectional one I would say, even though the concept was not widely established at that time.

In her critique, we find that these writers do not really unsettle the role of the teacher. Her critique focuses on the assumptions that make the basis of critical pedagogy, based in a Western humanist tradition. These assumptions set a classroom of rational individuals, meeting in dialogue, guided by shared universal moral ideas, and by a teacher who will help the students to raise their voice on their path to empowerment. A classroom of harmony and unity, fostering democratically engaged citizens.

Her main point is that the rationalism that works as the basis for

---

124 See for example the discussion in Gayatri Spivak "Righting wrongs", 2004.

125 Elizabeth Ellsworth, "Why Doesn't This Feel Empowering? Working Through the Repressive Myths of Critical Pedagogy," *Harvard Educational Review* 59, no. 3 (1989): 297–324.

critical pedagogy, and the rules of reason that the critical pedagogue enforces, work as a dominant and repressive force that does not support all the students in the classroom. "Rational argument has operated in ways that set up as its opposite an irrational Other, which has been understood historically as the province of women and other exotic Others."[126] This other is deemed irrational, and put in the category of inhabiting a naïve or magic consciousness.

Feminist post-structuralism exposes the violence carried out against these "others", and even though admittedly post-structuralism can work as dominant, it contextualizes pedagogy and asserts that knowledge is always partial. It allows for difference and conflict, also within the walls of the classroom, between students as well as between student and teacher. There is no safe space, no space out of reach of the power structures of the societies we are in. Even though critical pedagogy acknowledges the power imbalances between teacher and student, it does not intend to change them in any fundamental way. The teacher is still the one who knows how to know, who sets the framework of rational thought and dialogue.

Empowerment, in critical pedagogy, work as the concept that will bring the student up to the level of the teacher, leaving the authority of the teacher intact. The idea is that by providing analytic skills and student voice, the student will meet the teacher on equal terms as a free, rational individual. The idea of *student voice* in critical pedagogy is based on the idea that the teacher can help students express their subjugated knowledge, to voice it in the classroom dialogue.

But there are so many complex relations that silence a student, and there are many ways to speak. Speaking to survive, or talking back, as bell hooks have expressed in great detail[127], is not the same as *dialogue*. *Voice* in a feminist context is about a self-definition that is *in opposition* to that of the oppressors, a voice that puts the privileged position at risk. In a classroom the position of the professor is a position of privilege in itself, and the bodies that inherit that posi-

126 llsworth, 301.
127 bell hooks, *Talking Back - Thinking Feminist, Thinking Black*, vol. 2 (Boston: South End Press, 1989).

tion often come with other privileges as well – of maleness, whiteness, education, language, class and so on.

Ellsworth concludes that critical pedagogy does not sufficiently address the ways in which the teacher is implicated in the power structures they are trying to address. Even when it recognizes that everyone brings knowledge to the classroom, it insists on putting the teacher at the centre of knowledge, instead of recognizing that not only is the teacher's knowledge partial, it is also limited by their own implications in their social class and ties to the institution. There are things that the teacher from their position can never know.

The need for self-reflection in the teacher role

A way to address this would be to turn the idea of critical consciousness towards ourselves in our role as teachers. What is the critical consciousness of the teacher? And how can it be achieved? If we aim to work towards a more horizontal relationship between teacher and student, and towards a pedagogy that does not depend on linear progress, the process of attaining critical consciousness should not be one-sided or one-directional.

In bell hooks' writing this is a question of self-actualization. hooks' "engaged pedagogy" emphasizes education as a holistic endeavour, that encompasses the whole life and being of the student. Engaged pedagogy aims at well-being, and the role of the teacher corresponds to that of the healer. In this line of thought the healer cannot ignore their own well-being if they want to successfully heal others, and the teacher who wants to empower must herself be empowered. By working on her own self-actualization, she can teach from a place of self-awareness.[128]

hooks is immensely affected by Freire's work, and accounts for the impact he and his work has had on her teaching. Bringing together Freire's aim towards a liberation that makes all people fully human, and hooks' idea of a holistic education as an education for freedom, the question arises: how can we teach from a place that considers our full humanity? Not only the full humanity of students

128 hooks, *Teaching Community: A Pedagogy of Hope*, 179.

but also the full humanity of teachers. When the students in Freire's project are asked to grasp the conditions of their life and how it is connected to the society around them, then so are we. What are the structures that condition our lives, and our work as teachers? How does that impact the formation of our relations? How do we relate to the people, lives, objects and structures around us? How can we define our limit-situations, and how can we formulate the actions to transgress? I would consider these questions in relation to the actual teaching situation, as well as to our lives.

In Spivak I find contributions that are both more precise, and more expanded. In the extent of her writing, we can find that she insists that we are vigilant in examining ourselves and our position and relation to institutions. She insists that we are always complicit; to the institutions and the wider structures that uphold their power, and that we need to acknowledge our contamination and contextualize our claims[129]. This is done through a practice of self-implication, accountable reasoning and hyper-self-reflexivity.

Vanessa de Oliveira Andreotti helps us untangle what this entails. She argues that self-implication "entails an acute awareness of our complicity in historical and global harm through our inescapable investments in violent systems, such as modernity and capitalism."[130] In addition, accountable reasoning "means upholding an ethical responsibility to being aware of the reproduction of historical harm through the solutions we propose."[131] Finally, hyper-self-reflexivity "involves a constant engagement with three things: a) the social, cultural and historical conditioning of our thinking and of knowledge/power production; b) the limits of knowing, of language and of our senses in apprehending reality; and c) the non-conscious dynamics of affect (the fact that our traumas, fears, desires and attachments affect our decisions in ways that we often cannot identify)."[132]

Self-implication helps us remember our complicity and the need

129 Ilan Kapoor, "Hyper-Self-Reflexive Development? Spivak on Representing the Third World'Other'," *Third World Quarterly* 25, no. 4 (2004): 15.
130 de Oliveira (Andreotti), "Education, Knowledge and the Righting of Wrongs," 21.
131 de Oliveira (Andreotti), 21.
132 de Oliveira (Andreotti), 21.

to acknowledge it in the classroom, to name it. Even though we might address the students as intellectual equals, we are still there as representatives of the institution, however unfaithful we might be, and we are complicit in the upholding of those hierarchies. The students must not be allowed to forget. Often we have fought to even get into this classroom, to be allowed this position to teach, and in that struggle we are compelled to invest in the systems that uphold oppression/hierarchies. We take the right courses, we speak the right language, we gather the right credits. We assimilate to make a better fit. Now that we have arrived, it is not as easy to open the doors to others as we had expected. Without self-implication we might get stuck defending the investments we made in the system, and demand the same from others. We forget what we came here to do.

Accountable reasoning helps us examine our pedagogy, the solutions we propose. The harm that is done with good intentions. It helps us to take responsibility for our mistakes, to acknowledge and learn from them. It is hard to learn when you have done harm, but never as hard as being on the receiving end of it. Accountable reasoning helps us listen to and receive critique from students and others, and examine how we came to that action in the first place.

Hyper-self-reflexivity is the hardest one, I think. It may also be the part that is closest to critical consciousness, but expressed as continuous action more than a state of being. Hyper-self-reflexivity implies the unceasing, gritty and endless work of study, the simultaneous processes of learning and unlearning that have to happen for fundamental change. It demands an examination of our core believes. It suggests checking and re-checking our language, our sources, our pedagogies, the stories we keep re-telling, the relationships we have formed, the habits we lean on. The things we think we have figured out, the things we claim to know.

With these questions in mind, we can teach on unstable ground, on the edge of what we know, always directing the questions we pose to the students as much to ourselves. It encourages us to enter the classroom as a place to study, and to teach what we most need to learn. Maybe this could be a way of implementing the intentions behind Freire's idea of a teacher-student and student-teacher, where the roles start to unsettle. Doing this work of self-actualization or hyper-self-reflexivity suggests a shift towards the unknown, as it reveals our own limitations. But it also anchors us more firmly in our intentions, rather than our goals. We no longer need to claim to hold the truth, but we hold tight to our intentions and the way we form our invitations.

An attempt at displacing naïve and magic consciousness

Another way we can interrupt the linearity of critical consciousness theory, is to use the ideas of naïve and magic consciousness, not as the other that distinguishes the critical, but as simultaneously present facets of consciousness that complement each other. To make productive Freire's discarded notions of naïve and magic consciousness demands a rather radical and creative displacement of these terms[133]. Once displaced, they can work to supplement critical consciousness where it lacks in considering our whole humanity in its complexity.

Returning to the situations illustrated in *Teaching for Critical Consciousness*, looking at the first illustration[134], I see the man, front and centre. Barefoot in the field, with a tool in one hand and a book in the other, surrounded by nature; trees, birds and flowers on all sides. Behind him are the fruits of his labour; a house, a well, a woman and a child with their backs turned, faceless.

The discussion described in relation to the illustration talks about Man, and how Man makes the well, because he is thirsty; so he transforms the world, he makes culture – therefore he is subject.

---

133 Displacement is a strategical act that Spivak uses to make use of the knowledge from her own European education, with thinkers like Kant, Schiller and DeMan, by shifting the place of a concept or sentiment, and, as I read it, simultaneously lose control over it. It is an "intentional mistake". It is a freeing act. "I follow the conviction that I have always had, that we must displace our masters, rather than pretend to ignore them." Gayatri Chakravorty Spivak, *An Aesthetic Education in the Era of Globalization* (Cambridge, Massachusetts: Harvard University Press, 2012), 117–118 and 25.

134 *Freire, Education for Critical Consciousness.*
"FIRST SITUATION: Man in the World and with the World, Nature and Culture" drawing by Vicente de Abreu after originals by Francisco Brenand can be found on page 3 of the appendix. Also available online at http://aristotelesberino.blogspot.com/2017/10/paulo-freire-trama-das-imagens-entre-o.html

Through his work, through the transformation of nature to culture, he has made the world the object of his knowledge. These truths are established through dialogue with the students, prompted by questions like "Who made the well?", "Why did he do it?". In this dialogue, the woman and child are not mentioned.[135]

Within the framework of this situation, I am still able to imagine the woman's rituals of care; for the house, for the plants, for the child; her herb wisdom, her lullabies and spells in unwritten language. I imagine the child's never-ending questions, their unimpeded curiosity, picking up every rock, looking under every leaf, continuously surprised and ready to make the most ridiculous assumptions about the world. What would happen if they were included as subjects in this exercise? What if their relationship to nature was considered knowledge, and their practices considered culture?

According to Freire, with a naïve consciousness, you have some insight into your situation, but you are not able to turn that knowledge into action. You are unable to see the structures and make the connections necessary. This might be true. But if we displace this idea, from considering it an early stage in a linear development, to being a present aspect of our consciousness, it will still be limited in its view, but come with potential. Naïve could mean seeing things anew. It has within it an awe of the world. Naïve comes before hierarchies, all is equally fascinating, big and small. It may offer us a hint of what it was like before we were educated, the thought process of an unlearned mind. It might even be able to support us in a process of unlearning.

A naïve consciousness could be developed through a praxis (the combination of action and reflection) of *astonished contemplation*[136], marked by fascination and appreciation. It is not a place we want to be in all the time, but it has its uses. Like the first time you learned

135 Freire, *Education for Critical Consciousness*. page 4 of the appendi

136 *"Astonished contemplation" is a term coined by Ernst Bloch to capture the philosophical mode of contemplating the world from a sense of awe. See Ernst Bloch, The Principle of Hope Volume I (Cambridge, Massachusetts: MIT Press, 1953) and José Esteban Muñoz, Cruising Utopia: The Then and There of Queer Futurity (New York, NY and London, UK: New York University Press, 2009).*

to develop copies in the photo lab, and every copy seemed equally great, in their different ways. Before you learned what was considered good and bad, to differentiate in quality of expression. We do it when we brainstorm, in automatic writing, when we improvise in collaborations. We put our critical mind on pause to be able to roam the meandering pathways of our mind, without hesitation.

Teaching people in the very beginning of their studies of art, their awe of the art they come across can challenge our sense of authority. I have been provoked by students love of the generic paintings sold to tourists in the streets of Barcelona, of the posters at IKEA, of a skewed painting of a crying child. Their astonishment challenged my schooling of what is to be considered good and bad art, and unsettled the hierarchies of the art world I had learned to recognize. I have had to strip myself of that uniform and reconnect with my naïve consciousness in order to tune in to their excitement. This has been necessary to support their curiosity and exploration, and it has also helped me to reconnect with some interests that I lost on the way – of porcelain figurines, of still life paintings, of folklore embroidery.[137]

The downside of naïveté is that we have less ability to sort and make sense of what we encounter. But if we recognize that we are never past a naïve consciousness, then we can acknowledge that there are areas of life where we are still naïve, where we will have to tread carefully. We acknowledge that our knowledge is partial, and that others know more, however high up in the hierarchies we travel.

With a magic consciousness you assign all facts to a higher power, out of your control. According to Freire this renders you passive, you accept life as it is. To me, magical thinking is what we assign those who think beyond what is, beyond the rational and reasonable. "Magical" has been how indigenous knowledges, spiritual and religious (outside the accepted religion for that society) have been labelled, and with that label considered inferior. Granting access to our magic consciousness could include accepting that not every-

137 The example I am referring to here is Konstverkstad, see appendix.

thing is within our control – that there are powers in the works we do not completely understand. It could entail accommodating our spiritual connections, re-connecting with the knowledge of our elders, the knowledge of our community, with astrological knowledge, medicine and folklore. It could mean listening carefully to those stories that has lived with us for generations.

British anthropologist Susan Greenwood suggests that magic consciousness can and should be part of scientific thought. It could be seen as an alternative perception, a relational and holistic mode of cognition, inviting access to the non-material realm, where non-human beings have agency, vitality and spirit. Magic consciousness is characterised by an intense subjectivity that is not dissociated from the world, but rather "a practical participatory process of being"[138].

> "To my mind, the unfathomable is what happens when we let the magical imagination have full rein. It is a creative act, a chaotic act, we need to let go of our assumptions and engage in what might seem like madness. Plunging into the world of magic is a reawakening of strong imagination, a re-kindling of soul and a resistance to over-rationalization."[139]

MAGIC CONSCIOUSNESS can entail embracing the full capacities of our imagination. It can be seen as a possibility to honour Spivak's call to "keep up the work of displacing belief onto the terrain of the imagination"[140]. Imagination, in the case of Spivak, means "thinking absent things"[141]. It is the faculty (the capacity, the power) to make representations appear, with or without an external incitement. Imagination is a creative force of the psyche that stands in contrast to reason – it challenges our habits and teaches us to play. My sense

138 Susan Greenwood, "The Owl, the Dragon and the Magician: Reflections on Being an Anthropologist Studying Magic," *The Pomegranate Special Issue* Vol 17, no. 1–2 (2016): 145.

139 Greenwood, 153.

140 Spivak, *An Aesthetic Education in the Era of Globalization*, 10.

141 Spivak, 16.

is that imagination, in contrast to reason, is better at handling complex thought, to undo binary oppositions and to hold tension, without succumbing to either end of the pendulum.

Reinterpreted this way, naïve and magic consciousness do not need to be regarded as passive. But they differ from the critical in tempo and transparency; being too fast or too slow, being still, persistent, being unclear, muddy. They offer openings more than conclusions, maps rather than goals. Together they offer a more holistic perspective and a better chance to account for the full extent of our lives. We do not have to leave where we came from behind. Critical consciousness needs to be supplemented, with the naïve and the magical, not as opposites, but as facets that complement each other.

Double and mestiza/border consciousness

How can we unsettle the linearity of critical consciousness theory? Can we think about consciousness in multiple dimensions? I turn to the works of W.E.B. Du Bois and Gloria Anzaldúa as they provide openings to think about other dimensions of consciousness that act simultaneously, and often contradictory, to each other. In their work we can find the resources to examine both the borders and overlapping of consciousness.

W.E.B. Du Bois' notion of double consciousness comes out of his experience and analysis of the position of the black man in North America. Written in 1903, *The Souls of Black Folk* is a collection of essays that handle the specific conditions of living "as a Negro and as an American", and the painful process of coming to self-consciousness in this insoluble position.

> " ...born with a veil, and gifted with second-sight in this American world, – a world which yields him no true self-consciousness, but only lets him see himself through the revelation of the other world. It is a peculiar sensation, this double consciousness, this sense of always looking at one's self through the eyes of others, of measuring one's soul by the tape

> of a world that looks on in amused contempt and pity."[142]

IN DU BOIS' AMERICA, true self-consciousness is possible only for those who are white. Being placed behind a veil, there is no possibility to see oneself clearly. The picture is distorted by the gaze of hegemonic culture; he sees himself through the reflection of the other, at the same time as he tries to see himself. The two pictures are superimposed on top of each other so that none of them comes into focus. This results in a split sense of self, a division of the soul, to exist in the double bind of "two warring ideals in one dark body"[143].

This reveals how hard self-reflection gets when you are imbued in the consciousness of hegemonic culture, in what Freire calls the *oppressed consciousness*. Du Bois offers an insight into this experience from the position of the oppressed. But, contrary to Freire's linear vision of being lifted up and out of the oppressed consciousness, up to another level, to be freed from this position between cultures, Du Bois' vision is one of constantly striving to merge the two without losing either one. He presents double consciousness as a double bind. The strive to be one, to become whole, must not erase the Americanness, nor the blackness[144]. At the same time, the merge is inconceivable. What is left is the strive, to what Spivak would call "supplement the gap"[145].

The gift and burden of Du Bois second-sight, is that of seeing differently, of seeing from a position of difference, through a double lens. The origins of second sight has spiritual connotations; it is the birth sign of being born with a caul covering the infants face, believed to signal that the child will have prophetic and psychic gifts. The caul being another representation of the veil[146]. This sug-

---

142 W.E.B Du Bois, *The Souls of Black Folk*, Oxford World's Classics (Oxford: Oxford University Press, 2007), 8.
143 Du Bois, 8.
144 Du Bois, 9.
145 Spivak, *An Aesthetic Education in the Era of Globalization*, 98.
146 Du Bois, *The Souls of Black Folk*. in the explanatory notes.

gests that being born behind the veil is a burden, but it comes with powers that stretch into the future. It puts emphasis on the role of the oppressed as the ones who imagine otherwise, beyond the present. The oppressed sit with the capacity of future vision, with resources from both cultures to fuse into something new. Behind the veil, he starts to see a faint revelation of his power, and as he attempts the painful fusing of his own split soul, he will find the way to heal a divided society[147]. In this way, Du Bois has the same vision as Freire, that the oppressed, in liberating themselves will liberate all.

In *Borderlands/La Frontera: The New Mestiza,* Gloria Anzaldúa writes about life on the border. Mestiza culture balances on the border between northern Mexico and southern USA. Living with three cultures; the native American, the Mexican and the white American, that contradict each other at the same time as they depend on and blend with each other, sets a certain living condition, that prompts the development of *a mestiza consciousness* – a consciousness of the Borderlands.

> "Because I, a *mestiza,*
> continually walk out of one culture
> and into another,
> because I am in all cultures at the same time,
> alma entre dos mundos, tres, cuatro,
> me zumba la cabeza con lo contradictorio.
> Estoy norteada por todas las voces que me hablan
> *simultaneamente."*[148]

TORN BETWEEN CULTURES, Anzaldúa initially finds herself in an emotional state of perplexity, insecurity and indecisiveness. But this position cannot stick. The need to take a counter stance to the dominance of White culture has put her in a defensive state, that restricts her ability to move. And she must be moving – walking *into*

147 Du Bois, 11.
148 Anzaldúa, *Borderlands/La Frontera: The New Mestiza*, 99.

and *out of*, simultaneously entering and exiting. So she decides to leave the realm of re-action, to move into the possibilities of acting. She develops the capacity to deal with ambiguity, uncertainty and contradiction. She learns to remain flexible, and to stretch her psyche horizontally and vertically, in a way that includes rather than excludes. She turns to divergent thinking, away from linearity, away from set patterns and goals, towards a more whole perspective. Operating in a pluralistic mode, where nothing is discarded, rejected or thrown out, she holds space for all of it: the good with the bad, the different languages, the dormant gods, the vivid cultures.[149]

Standing at a point where things tend to collide, *la mestiza* also holds the power to connect what has been separated. In this unifying process, this synthesis, a third element occurs that is the mestiza consciousness. It is more than the sum of its parts. This process is a painful one, and takes immense effort and creativity. It consists of a massive uprooting of dualistic thinking in the individual and collective consciousness, and strives to heal the split that is the foundation of our lives.[150]

Anzaldúa makes a parallel between *la mestiza* and the queer; both are on the border and crossing the border simultaneously. Both are challenging dichotomies. As queers are part of any class and any culture, their role is to connect different cultures, by carrying knowledge across borders, from one culture to another[151]. She also connects the struggle of the *mestiza* with that of "the females, the homosexuals of all races, the dark skinned, the outcast, the persecuted, the marginalized, the foreign"[152] but before we come together, we need to know the history of each other's struggles. With this historically situated knowledge, the real struggle can begin, and it is an inner struggle, a struggle of the soul.

Anzaldúa portraits the oppressed as not being numbed by the violence and oppression that they have been subjected to. She affirms their ability to tap into their experience as a resource, as a

149 Anzaldúa, 77–80.
150 Anzaldúa, 80–81.
151 Anzaldúa, 106–7.
152 Anzaldúa, 60.

certain form of intelligence, or capacity – a faculty. *La faculdad* is the unconscious ability to sense the structures below the surface of things. It is a felt sense, a knowing without words, expressed in symbols and images. It does not reside in reason, but in the body.

The oppressed are forced to develop this faculty as a form of survival tactic. At first, it develops out of fear for one's safety, one's life, and appears as a heightened awareness of one's surroundings, a readiness for any sense of danger. At its second state, it cuts deeper, developing the ability to look through things, seeing behind the surface, into the depths. *La faculdad* is "anything that breaks into one's everyday mode of perception, that causes a break in one's defences and resistance, anything that takes one from one's habitual grounding, causes the depth to open up, causes a shift in perception"[153]. This faculty is latent in all of us.

Anzaldúa speaks directly to the oppressors as well, to the gringos, the Whites. They too have a dual consciousness, but a duality built on ignoring parts of their own history, splitting of parts of themselves. Dividing things into opposites; good-bad, male-female, white-black, American-Mexican and chopping of the bad half of the two. Not recognizing what they have deemed "the other" as their shadow. Hiding behind contempt they refuse to acknowledge their interdependency with people living on the same land. She says "Gringo, accept the doppelganger in your psyche. By taking back your collective shadow the intracultural split will heal. And finally, let us know what you need from us."[154] With this statement Anzaldúa makes an invitation. The oppressed become the teachers or the healers, the one's who carry knowledge and wisdom, and the oppressors become the students who need to study.

At the same time, these categories tend to blur. When teaching from *Borderlands*, it has been apparent how we identify with both the *mestiza* and the gringo, both the oppressed and the oppressor, depending on where our lives play out at that moment, and what parts of ourselves we can access. She also opens up the intersec-

153 Anzaldúa, 61.
154 Anzaldúa, 108.

tional possibility to recognize all the different facets of our identity – to sexuality, class and gender, as well as to the cultures we've inherited from previous generations. This does not free us from the responsibility of the oppressors or the privileged. On the contrary, she encourages us to dig deep, and to do the painful work of acknowledging the harm that we have done, and keep on doing, to set the foundation to make change possible.

Both *second sight* and *la faculdad* are developed as a response to oppression. The long-term pressure on the soul has turned out diamonds: gifts in the form of knowledge as well as a way of being, a skill of comprehension, a consciousness. These forms of consciousness are raised to resist the matrix of domination[155] and oppose the status quo.

They can be said to be forms of split *consciousness*, that emerge from a conscious break with dominant ideology while remaining located within it[156]. For Du Bois, double-consciousness cannot accept the systemic humiliation of the Black man. His focus of opposition is the strive to merge the double images into one where one can be both Black and American. This strive is a political one (the ballot, education and work) as well as a merging of the soul. He has a vision for America that opposes the colour line, the racist separation of peoples living on the same land, "... in order that some day on American soil two world-races may give each to each those characteristics both so sadly lack"[157].

Anzaldúa's double consciousness opposes the relentless sexism, homophobia and racism of both Chicano/a culture and White America. Her work is an affirmation of the situation she is in, and the knowledge she has developed from this situation. Her consciousness reflects her life in the borderlands; being on the border, on the crossroads, balancing the different cultures, holding the ambiguities of multiple voices and cultures.

---

155 Patricia Hill Collins, *Black Feminist Thought: Knowledge, Consciousness, and the Politics of Empowerment* (New York, NY: Psychology Press, 2000).

156 Chela Sandoval, *Methodology of the Oppressed* (Minneapolis: University of Minnesota Press, 2000), 84.

157 Du Bois, *The Souls of Black Folk*, 13.

A split consciousness acts from a place of resistance and opposition, engaging difference as a creative and powerful force. It does not take away from the hegemonic view of the world, but adds another dimension that the subject has to deal with simultaneously and often contradictory.

Both Du Bois and Anzaldúa are opposing a Western logic of binaries and separation. Freire's work is built on the separation of ignorant from knowing, of human from animal, of nature from culture and of the critical from the naïve and magical. In Du Bois' and Anzaldúa's work there is no possibility of separating from the cultures that form their lives. Their strive takes another route, to deal with the situation as it is, with all its contradictions and ambiguities.

Second sight and la faculdad suggest a capacity to see deeper, beyond the surface of things. Seeing deeper is not the same as seeing clearly. Deeper unearths structures, but they are still muddy, still complex. Digging to the root of things does not make things clear and easy. It reveals the complex interconnections and extensible patterns, with no clear beginnings and no clear ends. It is not a question of either or, but this and more.

Du Bois' and Anzaldúa's work supports us in examining the borders and overlapping of consciousness. They support the idea that the development of one's consciousness is a continuous process, that holds contradictions and double vision. The veil has not been lifted, and it does not have to be. Confronted with their thinking, a critical consciousness could be superimposed with the naïve and the magical, or at a crossroads with them. Their work encourages us to hold on to ambiguity, to hold on to the contradicting parts of ourselves and the different cultures we are a part of. As teachers we can recognize this in ourselves, as well as in the students. And strive for "a consciousness of multiple voices and paradigms"[158].

Experimenting with a pedagogy for a multifaceted consciousness

158 Theresa A Martinez, "The Double-Consciousness of Du Bois & The 'Mestiza Consciousness' of Anzaldúa," *Race, Gender & Class* Vol.9, no. 4 (2002): 171.

Based on the theory outlined above, I want to make the claim that we, as radical teachers, have the possibility to strive for a pedagogy that supports a critical consciousness that is non-linear, that holds plurality and contradiction. We can find pedagogies that help us support the development of a more conscious living in the students, from their particular position, in a plurality of ways, that do not encourage sameness, but difference. And, that acknowledges that this is a painful process, that takes a lot of courage and creativity.

We can encourage students to do the inventory of their own lives; the ancestry, the storytelling, the creation story of their culture(s). We can ask them to identify what borders they have crossed, and what borders they are still balancing. We can support them in picturing the contradictions, ambiguities and conflicts of their lived identities, to find the symbols and imagery to lean on, and we can prompt them to create, draw, write and sing from that place of consciousness.

Simultaneously, we will ask ourselves the very same questions. As teachers, we can position ourselves on much more unstable ground when we teach, in the contradictions of our own life story and where it has brought us. How we tell stories to ourselves will influence how we tell them to others. If we share the contradictions of our own lives, and not just what we have overcome, it will open much more possibility to connect. We can teach from the acknowledgement that the students have access to so much knowledge that is out of our reach.

Double and border consciousness hold a specific knowledge, but we all have the capacity to learn. Not by co-opting the experience of Du Bois or Anzaldúa, but by retracing and taking seriously our own suppressed knowledges and history, and find the blind spots, the dirty tracks, the borders we crossed, the unsolved tensions, the double vision, the blurry edges. It encourages us to speak with the ghosts of our own history and take on the hard task of looking and not distancing ourself from our shadow.

Enstrangement

As an example, I, like most of us, live in a different place than where

I grew up. I have moved about 1000 kilometres within the borders of the Swedish nation state. I may feel that I have made the choice to relocate by my own free will; I wanted to move away, to experience something bigger, to be in the city, in a university, to not be left behind, to find a more exciting job, to meeting exciting people. I may think that this is my individual story, not a story of peoples. But if I look carefully, many of my stories are the same as that of a generation or a people; a wave of migration from the countryside to the city, from the inland to the coast, from north to south. We are told not to identify as migrants, though we have migrated, we have crossed borders (though often unrecognized ones), we have travelled from a place that is considered less to a place that is considered more. Our stories line up with the official story; the settler colonial story of the kingdom and the colonies, the social democratic story of the rationality of equality and social progress, the capitalist story of efficiency and economic growth.

We have contributed with our bodies to the continuous stream from margin to centre.[159]

In this process we are encouraged to leave something behind, to hide or cut off parts of ourselves that seem incompatible with the new. We have centralized, adapted ourselves, urbanized. We have rid ourselves of what is considered lesser cultures – of the working class, of the rural folks – to fit neatly in the middle. We now have acquired great taste and great values. We have rid ourselves of dialect and we are articulate. We fit in. We pass. I pass.

I wrote a guided meditation for an event at MUMOK in Vienna that tried to deal with this issue. I wanted to address the travels we

159 Just to be clear, I am talking here about migration in a general sense, not to be confused with the experience of being a refugee, of which I have no experience. UNHCR offers this definition: "Refugees are persons fleeing armed conflict or persecution. Migrants choose to move not because of a direct threat of persecution or death, but mainly to improve their lives by finding work, or in some cases for education, family reunion, or other reasons. Unlike refugees who cannot safely return home, migrants face no such impediment to return. If they choose to return home, they will continue to receive the protection of their government."
Refugees, United Nations High Commissioner for. "UNHCR Viewpoint: 'Refugee' or 'Migrant' – Which Is Right?" UNHCR. Accessed March 4, 2021. https://www.unhcr.org/news/latest/2016/7/55df0e556/unhcr-viewpoint-refugee-migrant-right.html.

have made to come to this place, at this time. I wanted to remind ourselves of the compromises, and often sacrifices, we have had to make to fit into this building, into this evening and its art world context. At the same time, I wanted the participants to pay attention to something that they brought with them from where they came from, something hidden, but precious and powerful. This recognition was aimed both at themselves, but also at recognizing that everyone in this room brought something wilfully or unwillingly concealed.

The work *Enter/Exit – a guided meditation to the point of no return* (2015) is centred on the walk from the subway station to the MUMOK museum and down to the room where the real-life event takes place. An imitation of the walk the participants just did. It starts off with reminding you of how you came to Europe and to Vienna, by posing a series of questions, that eventually puts you in the role of the protagonist, standing on the stairs that take you up from the subway and into the busy street.

The surroundings are described in a way that makes them a bit alien or strange, as if the protagonist is new to this place. The imagery has an added sense of intensity or sensory overload, where what is close to you or most immediate demands your attention, like it is the first time you encounter them. The journey takes you past the wall that surrounds the Museum Quarter, through the entrance and to the square in front of the MUMOK. The space is described as well as your sensory experiences of heat and smells:

> " *A cream coloured wall is stretching out on your left side. You start walking, following the wall. You are looking for a place to enter, an opening. The sunlight is reflecting from the wall, making the sidewalk bright and warm. Big signs get your attention and point you in the right direction. This is the main entrance. Three arches divided by pillars. You turn your back to the traffic and choose to enter through the middle archway. Somehow it seems appropriate.*
> *On the other side of the wall, the space opens up to a big square the size of a football field. The square is flanked on each side*

by two huge cubes. To your left is a white cube, big as a six-storey building. To you right an equally big cube in dark grey. Stone cubes. They seem like enclosed objects, resting heavy on the ground. Stairs that are leading up to a tiny entrance reveal that they are actually buildings."

Excerpt from *Enter/Exit*
– a guided meditation to the point of no return (2016)

THE AIM HERE, is to present this mundane walk with a heightened sensibility to the strangeness of the everyday, and later on, the strangeness of the particular space that is "the art world". The places, people and customs that hold the contemporary art scene together.

This process can best be described as *enstrangement* (*ostraniene* in Russian)[160] as it was first coined in 1917 by literary theorist Viktor Shklovsky in his essay Art as Device[161]. Enstrangement is an artistic device that makes the familiar unfamiliar, by looking at it from an unpredictable angle, or with an unexpected language. Shklovsky uses Leo Tolstoy's writing to exemplify his thesis: "The devices by which Tolstoy enstranges his material may be boiled down to the following: he does not call a thing by its name, that is, he describes it as if though it has been perceived for the first time, while an incident is described as if it where happening for the first time."[162] Other ways of attaining enstrangement might be by telling the story from an unexpected point of view, or describing objects with such detail, and with such words that are not usually associated with the object, that they become de-familiarized.

The aim of enstrangement is to make people *see* the object, not merely recognize it. According to Shklovsky, our perception of the familiar has become marked by automatism, a state of perception that is habitual and disengaged. "And so, held accountable for noth-

160 Ostraniene is a Russian neologism, which translator Benjamin Sher renders as "enstrangement." A thorough examination of the translation of ostraniene can be found in Alexandra Berlina's foreword to her translation of Shklovsky's text (Duke University Press, 2005).

161 Viktor Shklovsky, "Art as Device," in *Theory Of Prose* (London: Kalkey Archive Press, 1991).

162 Shklovsky, 6.

ing, life fades into nothingness. Automatization eats away at things, at clothes, at furniture, at our wives, and at our fear of war."[163] We stop seeing and experiencing things, they pass through us, unnoticed (even our wives!). But art has, with the device of enstrangement, this possibility to remove our tendency towards automatism, by slowing down our perception and making us stay with it – feel it, sense it, experience it.

This should not, however, be confused with Bertolt Brecht's *Verfremdungseffekt*, translated to "estrangement effect". This process of defamiliarization might seem similar at first, but Brecht's aim was that of emotional distance, for the audience to reflect on what was being presented in critical and objective ways, and this effect was implemented mainly by breaking with the illusion of theatre, revealing parts of the structure behind the presentation. Enstrangement is a process in the opposite direction, adding a veil of illusion to the everyday, so that one has to squint one's eyes, concentrate and focus, to understand what one is seeing. It is a matter of a change in intensity and awareness.

In a guided meditation, using enstrangement makes it possible for us to examine what we have started to take for granted or accept as a given. It reminds us how we looked at things when they were new to us, before we learned how to decode the signs around us, and put them in the appropriate context, box or hierarchy. It offers us an opportunity to practice our capacity for astonished contemplation.

When we are full of awe and every detail is equally fascinating, it opens us up to our naïve consciousness. To look at the world in wonder is to look at the world in vulnerability, with a radical openness to the magnificence of the world. This is what astonishment does for us. To contemplate on the world with an openness to being astonished, is an openness to being touched and changed by the encounter. To be full of awe to what is bigger and brighter than the scope of our limited senses. Uncontainable, incomprehensible. Astonishment ties to the radical admission that there is something bigger than us, that we are not to cool to be impressed, we welcome impressions. We want to be changed by encountering the others in the

163 Shklovsky, 5.

world. We will not be afraid.

To be in awe is to stop in your tracks. What astonishes us can be intimidating and unsettling. Unsettling a comfortably sorted and reasonable view of the world, where everything fits. The astonished event questions the choices you have made as it shows more possibilities than you had imagined. This break in the master narrative hosts a possibility of questioning the limits of our society. We can practice being astonished. We can foster attentiveness to awesomeness. We can stop and smell the flowers and allow ourselves to be amazed by the complex system and chance encounter that made this flower bloom with such intensity in colour and enchanting smell.

The symbolic object

In *Enter/Exit – a guided meditation to the point of no return*, a stone is introduced as an object you keep hidden in your pocket. You can feel it with your fingers. It is an object that is well known to you, as if you have carried it for a while. It gives you some comfort, but you are also anxious that it will be revealed. The properties of the stone are not described, nor the reasons why you carry it around.

An inner dialogue follows the meditation, about the efforts and the long journey you have made to get here, both physically and socially and about you're worries for not fitting in. The voice gives you assurance that you are OK, that you belong and are granted access.

In the end, you are quite at ease. You take a seat in the black box where the actual meditation takes place, and the meditation is superimposing the fiction on the actual present. The voice instructs you to take the stone out of your pocket.

There is a moment of anticipation. You have arrived at your destination and will fulfil your destiny. The voice suggests that a dramatic change will come, with destruction and new beginnings. And that you hold the power in your hand. In the end, you "release the stone". There is silence. After a pause you are brought back to the present.

The stone in this case, is mainly a symbol of the place, the land, you came from and maybe left behind. It represents loss and memory as well as a promise, a gift, a mission, a destiny. It holds a connection between past-present-future. Picking up stones and carrying them around is a well spread practice when people travel, to bring a piece of land from one place to the other. The stone can also be a representation of the earth, of a history that stretches way back, long before human life walked its surface, and will continue long after. Stones come as asteroids and meteorites. Stones are loaded with godly powers in many native religions, just as sacred stones can be found in all the major religions, and are used for their healing powers, as altars or Gods.

When the protagonist takes out the stone to release its hidden powers, the power of the stone is purposefully not too well defined. It carries tension. It is a burden and a promise. It is something you bring with you from the past, with the power to tear down the structures of the present, but the constitution of that power needs to be filled in by the participant. The future is left open, but the urgency of change is inevitable.

This part of the meditation invites the participant to fill the object of the stone with magical properties. Using the simple act of carrying a stone, there is opportunity to project both big and small features onto it. The sense of a stone is familiar and accessible, recognizable to the senses of touch, smell and even taste, at the same time as it carries the weight of symbolic value. The object acts as a portal to the magic consciousness. The suggestion of hidden powers in the stone indicates that the protagonist has capacities within them that have not been fully realised. Releasing the power of the stone releases some of that magical power.

Interruptions

The guided meditations I have made all contain elements of interruption. All teaching involves some form of manipulation, or coercion, however soft it comes across. Guided meditations hold the participants/students attention in a way that encompasses not only their conscious thoughts, but their unconscious and bodily sensations. I need the interruptions to make room for resistance. They form breaks in the continuum, where the participant becomes aware of themselves and the situation they are in. Being aware, they have the possibility to continue saying yes to my suggestions, or to refuse them. In the case of refusal, they can simply open their eyes and still follow along, still listening, but not fully engaging.

Inserting interruptions is an essential pedagogical tool. The focus on student centred education sometimes gives the impression that we are supposed to simply let the students follow whatever path or direction that comes naturally, without resistance. As Biesta has pointed out, putting up resistance is crucial to interrupt the status quo. For him, interruption has to do with provoking the student to de-centre themselves, for the purpose of being "in the world, without being in the centre of the world"[164]. He asks them to question if what they desire is desirable – for their own life, for their life with others, for the world, in a version of Spivak's "uncoercive rearrangement of desires"[165]. This interruption of desires is not about judging or suppressing their desires, or telling them what they should desire instead, but about bringing in these questions as a possibility. It pushes them to imagine themselves as active subjects in the world. Of being and becoming with the world.

The interruptions can work as a trigger for our critical consciousness. They force us to stop and look at the very situation we are in. In the guided meditations the interruptions take the form of changes in tempo, breaks in the narrative, symbolic thresholds and physical challenges. In *Unsettling II: A guided meditation to the sea,* the participants are guided to go into their body and follow the traction of gravity towards the building, the city of Venice, and the sea that the city rests on; there is a moment when the participants go in the water. At first it is a soothing experience of letting go, of falling slowly into the deep. This is interrupted with a moment where they are asked to put in the effort to adapt to the sea; to suppress their natural instinct to hold their breath, to let the sea water into their lungs:

164 Biesta, *The Rediscovery of Teaching*, 98.
165 Spivak, *An Aesthetic Education in the Era of Globalization*, 373.

Now it is time

to assimilate to the environment

and adapt our breathing to the ocean

You came from water, remember?

Your body is adaptable

you are prone to change

You can live in water

you did so for months

you just need to remind yourself

We're going to take a deep breath together

with force

breathing liquid into our lungs

3, 2, 1 and

(in)

Let the water pass your lips, your mouth, your throat, down your lungs

take it in (in)

Feel the taste of salt, tearing at your throat

the burn that hits your lungs

let it burn

This burn will sustain you

you will live in this pain

we are together in this pain

This is the necessary connection

of living body to body

Water in, water out

Suffering is essential

just hold on

Keep on breathing

one breath at a time

Focus on the rhythm

of natural breath

it will keep you alive

You are breathing water

We are breathing water

Water is life

Water is life

Excerpt from *Unsettling II: A guided meditation to the sea* (2017)

AT THIS MOMENT the sound intensifies and picks up tempo. It is not meant to be easy, it is meant to be a challenge, to take some effort, and that demands a decision to be made: do you want to continue? The interruption gives space to critically examine the situation, to question what is. In contrast to the promise of peace of mind of more traditional meditations, the interruptions are meant to trigger the participant's agency, the will to act with intent. The decision to engage is a returning commitment during the meditation.

A pedagogy of interruptions can also be turned towards the institution. We are always teaching the institutions as well, do we not? As an example, I can share a project I was involved in that included both a school and a museum[166]. The museum wanted to reach parts of the population that were under-represented in their audience, namely young people whose parent were not part of the white, Swedish born middle class. In this project, the students were invited to curate an exhibition with works from the main collection, as part of their studies. These kinds of projects are often presented as an exception, on the side of the main event, and as pedagogical projects more than art. To interrupt this logic, we introduced a restriction on all the involved staff, from curators to technicians and teachers. They were not allowed to use two of the words most commonly used in this kind of project; "ungdomar" which translates to "young people" or "youngsters", and "duktig" which is what you say to a child that is performing well, or is well behaved. The students involved in the project were adults, so the use of "ungdomar" was mainly a derogatory term, to separate them from students of the

166 See appendix Konstverkstad

university, or the grown-ups working at the museum, though the age span sometimes overlapped. The other word, "duktig", is a positive affirmation, but its prerequisite is unequal: it is said by someone who knows to the one who do not know. It is a jargon to separate the project from the established operations of the museum. We continuously had to remind each other to find other, better words, that took seriously the position and knowledge of the students. In this case, it was necessary to interrupt the institution's usual language, to open the possibility for a different language and another relation to develop.

Unfinishedness

How can the concept of critical consciousness still hold value to us as radical teachers? The concept of critical consciousness is useful to support the critical examination of the stories we are told, as well as the stories we tell ourselves. It reminds us to resist the truth told by power, and examine the systems and relations that hold power in place. At the same time, we will recognize that the critical part of our mind is not the only valid form of consciousness. It can be supplemented with awe of naïve and magical thinking. We can learn to balance on the border of different modes of thinking, and recognize when they overlap and blur our vision. In leaving the idea of awakening behind, and with it the linear narrative of a before and after, we will free the student from being the object of liberation, and the teacher from the role of the liberator, and trust that we all still have a role to play.

We will not pretend that we are freed from the pitfalls of critical, naïve or magical thinking. We will look out for passivity or evasiveness, for universalist strivings, for arrogance and projection, for the critical distance that keeps us from our ability to engage.

This process of learning is never finished. We will never awaken to a "true" consciousness, or a perfect state of knowing. In his later work, Freire adds *unfinishedness* as a part of the human condition:

> " It is in our incompleteness, of which we are aware, that education as a permanent process is grounded.

> Women and men are capable of being educated only to the extent that they are capable of recognizing themselves as unfinished. Education does not make us educable. It is our awareness of being unfinished that makes us educable. And the same awareness in which we are inserted makes us eternal seekers. Eternal because of hope. Hope is not just a question of grit or courage. It's an ontological dimension of our human condition.!"[167]

UNFINISHEDNESS, to Freire, means that as human beings, our lives are not predetermined and our destinies are not given. We will have to construct our lives and take responsibility for them. Our lives are conditioned, that is, there are set conditions for our lives in the genetic factors that we have inherited, as well as the socio-cultural and historical factors. There are people and systems that have power over us, but in the end, our lives are not decided for us. They are still unfinished.

Our awareness of this unfinishedness makes us insert ourselves into a permanent process of searching. It is our awareness of being unfinished that makes us open to the process of study. It reveals to us our ignorance, as well as that there is still much we can come to know.

Freire's recognition of our unfinishedness displays an openness to the unknown, and a step away from the definiteness of some of his earlier statements. Instead of relying on the strive for a "true" consciousness as a driving force of study, it is the recognition that we will never be truly knowledgeable that keeps us in the search. This version of being human stands on more uncertain ground, and is closer to a state of readiness than one of completion. This later work of Freire, has a more sensuous and intimate tone, and I propose this last passage to be read as an affirmation:

---

167 Paulo Freire, *Pedagogy of Freedom – Ethics, Democracy, and Civic Courage* (Lanham: Rowman & Littlefield Publishers, 2000), 42.

"I know that my passing through the world is not predetermined, preestablished.

That my destiny is not a given but something that needs to be constructed and for which I must assume responsibility.

I like being human because I am involved with others in making history out of possibility, (...)

Consequently, the future is something to be constructed through trial and error (...)

I like to be human because in my unfinishedness I know that I am conditioned. Yet conscious of such conditioning,

I know that I can go beyond it"[168]

168 Freire, 38.

INDUCTION:
An Unknown at the Heart of Our Lives[169]

We will end with a place to start.

169 "The intrusion of this type of transcendence, which I am calling Gaia, makes a major unknown, *which is here to stay*, exist at the heart of our lives." Isabelle Stengers, *In Catastrophic Times: Resisting the Coming Barbarism* (Lüneburg: Open Humanities Press, meson press, 2015), 47.

This is an invitation to a practice, an induction, in the form of a text[170]. I take the word induction from hypnotherapy and the teachings of Milton H. Erickson, as a series of suggestions that, if accepted, will lead one to a trance-like state[171]. The concept of trance, for Erickson, is not something extra-ordinary, it is the equivalent of daydreaming, staring out the window, or the flow that comes from intense exercise or creative work[172]. It is a state that we, under the right conditions, can access by ourselves. The trance state is useful because it is an adaptive state[173]: "a state of increased awareness and responsiveness to ideas"[174]. It opens a path to the unconscious, giving us a chance to take a look at those deep-set ideas and beliefs about ourselves and the world that we do not usually access or question.

The aim of this practice is to bring together two theoretical texts into an embodied practice, by using techniques from hypnotic induction and guided meditation. The texts that I have chosen, one by Isabelle Stengers and one by the Gesturing Towards Decolonial Futures Collective[175], offer us two powerful imageries that capture the structure of modernity and its destabilization, sparked by the current climate crisis. Imagery that begs a response. I have chosen to stay close to the original texts, breaking them up to allow more space for body and breath. Rewriting them this way is an attempt at offering an embodied way of approaching theoretical texts and is part of my pedagogical effort to engage our bodies in our understanding of this moment. It stems from my conviction that to be able to engage in the future unknown, we will have to bring our full

---

170 A version of this chapter was previously published as Lisa Nyberg, "INDUCTION: An Unknown at the Heart of Our Lives," Periskop: Forum for Kunsthistorisk Debat, no. 24 (2020): 48–61.

171 Rosen, *My Voice Will Go with You: The Teaching Tales of Milton H. Erickson*.

172 Erickson and Rossi, "Two-Level Communication and the Microdynamics of Trance and Suggestion," 18.

173 Webber and Thomas, "Talking Therapy Ep. 28 Dr. Jeffrey Zeig on the Evolution of Psychotherapy."

174 Erickson, "Pediatric Hypnotherapy," 129.

175 You can find the work of the Gesturing Towards Decolonial Futures collective at https://decolonialfutures.net/

selves, all that we can make intelligible: every sense, every cell, every process, every connection.

This practice is a pedagogical experiment in using text to perform the role of the guide or the teacher. The text works as a score, an instruction, a guide. Since I cannot be present with you, the reader, I have had to find a way to guide you from afar. The materiality of this practice is a text printed on paper–you can hold the words in your hands. While reading I will ask you to engage your senses in the service of imagination. I will invite you to drop down into your body: to follow the traction of gravity and connect with the body that is you, and with the body of Earth that you rest on. The being that encompasses all the complex relations of land, sea, soil and atmosphere, and all the dead and living things that together make Gaia.

Gaia is one of the Greek primordial deities. She is the personification of the Earth, the ancestral mother of all life, the goddess Mother Earth. In the story told by Isabelle Stengers, Gaia is she who intrudes[176]. She is making her presence known as an entity in her own right. Not simply a symbolic other, but a person to be reckoned with: a powerful other–a mother that is not only there to nourish and protect us, but who is a person with her own mind, intruding into the man-made order of things, bringing chaos, or calling back a lost order.

Stengers names her a being, some*thing* that becomes some*one* who is more than the sum of her processes[177]. Gaia is a person equipped with history, activity, and sensitivity. This being holds together a complex set of processes and relations in a way that has so far been in our favour, but might not be any longer. She has left behind her traditional role as a caretaker and stepped into her power to question us all. She is not holding it together[178], she is letting go.

Gaia is ticklish. When we disturb her, she responds with disproportionate measures, shrugging us off like irritating bugs[179]. Our

176 Stengers, *In Catastrophic Times: Resisting the Coming Barbarism*.
177 Stengers, 44–45.
178 Stengers, 45.
179 Stengers, 46.

actions as human beings have provoked a cascade of unforeseeable responses. We depend on her – she tolerates us. We must pay attention not to offend her[180]. This induction is an invitation to feel the impact of Gaia's intrusion: on our habitat, on our houses, on our bodies.

Naming her Gaia is an act of imagination. "To name is not to say what is true but to confer on what is named the power to make us feel and think in the mode that the name calls for."[181] Stengers offers us this powerful being, Gaia, to think and feel with. She gives flesh to what seems un-graspable; she gives us a presence to witness, a body to connect with, a person to speak to; she offers us the possibility of using our imagination to build a relationship with the complex and powerful processes that the Earth holds.

Naming, for Paulo Freire, is a pedagogical act in the service of liberation. In his quest for the oppressed to be more fully human, the power to *name the world* is essential for stepping into the agency that is central to claiming one's humanity. Dialogue stands at the center of Freire's pedagogical theory, and dialogue demands of us to speak a *true word*–a word that contains both the element of action and reflection[182]. A word that performs. A word that transforms. Naming is in this case a creative act, an act of creation, of adding to the story of our world.

Naming is not a finite act. "Once named, the world in its turn reappears to the namers as a problem and requires of them a new naming"[183]. Gaia who intrudes will return to us to be re-named, over and over again, as we engage in the transformation of our world. In this practice, we are purposefully aiming away from the colonial act of naming to claim power over others by ways of categorization and systematization. Naming is not made to label, sort, and place into hierarchies. We aim to use naming as a performative act: to give life, form, and space to what we need to imagine otherwise.

The Gesturing Towards Decolonial Futures Collective gives name

180 Stengers, 62.
181 Stengers, 43.
182 Freire, *Pedagogy of the Oppressed*, 88.
183 Freire, 69.

and form to the pillars of Western epistemology as "the house that modernity built"[184]. This house is our home and our minds' prison. We encounter the world from a place that is built on separation, with two carrying walls, one of universal reason built on enlightenment humanism, one of the modern nation state, and a heavy roof of capitalism that threatens to overwhelm the house with endless growth. This house is not well. I have placed this house on the surface of Gaia to establish the connection between our human-made environmental crisis and the cultures that provoked it. Not all humans have brought on the intrusion of Gaia – it is not "humanity" that is responsible, it is certain human cultures. Gaia intrudes because of the dominance of our Western culture(s), the systems they produce, and the privileged behaviours they encourage. Gaia intrudes because of what the house of modernity keeps teaching us: a desire for accumulation, growth and progress, for mastery and certainty, for consensus, coherence, and control.

Thankfully, we can change culture, shift our values and beliefs, and change our habits. We can do the work to dismantle capitalism, unsettle and decolonize our cultures, and imagine otherwise. Central to this transformation is an epistemological shift away from the epistemology of the house of modernity. This shift demands of us to reconsider what knowledge is, what is worth knowing, as well as what the purpose of knowing might be. It questions our desire, not for knowledge, but for *knowing*. For being the ones who know how to know[185]. For claiming certainty. Inspired by Spivak, this practice aims towards an "uncoercive re-arrangement"[186] of those desires towards more unstable, vulnerable, and arable grounds.

184 Vanessa Andreotti, Sharon Stein, and Rene Susa, "From the House That Modernity Built to Healthy Mycelium," *Decolonial Futures Collective*, 02072018, decolonialfutures.net.

185 Jacques Rancière, "Un-What?," in *The Pedagogics of Unlearning* (Earth, Milky Way: punctum books, 2016), 27.

186 Spivak, *An Aesthetic Education in the Era of Globalization*, 373.

Preparation

This text should be read in a place where you can be undisturbed. A place where you can feel safe enough to let go of what is going on around you, let attention drift and your mind wander. I will ask you to follow the dots on the page with your fingertip. For a more sensuous experience you can take a sharp pencil or needle and make little holes on each dot from the backside of the page. This way you will have small elevations in the paper that you can follow with your fingertip when you start reading.

Find yourself a comfortable position. You can sit in a chair, by a table, on a sofa, on a bed, or on the floor. Take off your shoes. Consider your level of energy. Make sure that you are warm enough for sitting still. You can use extra clothes or a blanket to support yourself, rolled up under your seat, behind your back, or over your shoulders or feet to keep warm.

Hold this text in your hand or lay it out on the table in front of you. Make sure your other hand is free to move over the page. Remember that you are free to shift and move around during this practice. There is no need to sit perfectly still. Stillness is not static. We aim for a focused attention and the ability to stay with the practice. Allowing for the body-mind to be, here, still.

Make an effort to slow down, to find a rhythm that is calmer than your day-to-day pace. You can pause, close your eyes, and take a breath whenever it is needed. When you are ready to continue, your fingertip will guide you back to the text.

Let's get started.

GOING IN

Let the air leave your body
and fill it up again
breathing
with intention
to bring oxygen and life
to all parts of your body
Breathing into
nose
sinuses
lungs
stomach

Breathe out tension
in your jaw
neck
shoulders
lower back
hips
Let the energy
of your breath
slip through the cavities in your hip bone
down your legs
and feet

Awaken your senses:
taste inside the mouth
the smells entering your nose
ears open in all directions
the sense of your clothes against your skin
light and colour caught by your eyes
the touch of your fingertip to this paper

Let your breath touch your heart
let it gently massage the cavities in your chest

to bring spaciousness and softness
around the heart

Search for all the points of connection
of your body to the surface beneath you
it might be your feet, your sit bones, your back
register the points of pressure
and how they differ in intensity

Notice how your body rests
supported
by the weave of the fabric
and the structure of the furniture
beneath you
Sense how the energy you produce is met with energy from below
reaching for you
to be touched
and held

The floor beneath you is connected to the walls
held in balance by the construction of the building
secured into the foundation of the house

sunken into the ground for stability
supported by soil and rock
Held in tension

by the curved surface of the Earth's crust
a connecting circle
the vastness of the globe beneath you

There she is
Gaia
the body on which you rest

Take a moment to imagine Gaia
to sense her presence
follow the circle by touch

GAIA

Gaia is a powerful being
a planet body
tumbling through space
hot lava at her core
a thin crust of soil
and a cool, bright atmosphere
protecting her surface from the rays of the Sun

We rest our bodies on her
her lap is our home
our den
our bit of luck in endless darkness
her soil is the place from which we grow

Appreciate the air entering your body
that it is safe and clean
not too warm or too cold
not too damp or too dry
How the thin atmosphere protects us from deep space
and the entire ecosystem
the whole being of Gaia
is engaged to keep the balance of oxygen to nitrogen
that is the air that we breathe

Studying the face of Gaia
you recognize the impact of anthropogenic climate change
the rising temperature
and how it is producing storms, droughts, heat waves, and thaw
You witness the rapid loss of life
as populations of species are getting heavily reduced

trapped on smaller and smaller habitats
surrounded by humanity's monocultures
You identify the plastic islands in the sea
and the microplastics in your drinking water

The continuation of human life on this Earth is not guaranteed
neither is life for most of our companion species
large populations of animals are already gone
the seabeds are suffocating
the ice is melting
methane gas is rising towards the surface
There are high levels of energy in the atmosphere
leading to extreme weather

You have experienced bad weather before
suffocating heat
pinching cold
winds that bully you
You have stood at the shore of roaring seas
you have felt the power of Gaia
you might think you know her

But this is another time
this storm will not pass to return next year
this cold will not be avoided indoors
this heat will not cool in the night
this flood will not return to sea

Take a second
to notice the rhythm of your pulse
and the tempo of your breath

THE HOUSE

On the surface of Gaia
there is a house
a familiar, square building
This is the house that modernity built[187]

Many of us grew up in this house
it fosterwed our view of the world
through the frames of its windows
Many of us grew up in its shadow
and adapted our lives in response to its needs and demands

On one side there is a carrying wall
built with the bricks from Enlightenment humanism
it is the wall of universal reason
that teaches us to sort our knowledge in straight lines of logic
first this, then that,
either or, neither nor
It teaches us to separate what our bodies know
from what our minds can comprehend

On the other side is a carrying wall
built on the principles of liberal rights and justice
it is the wall of the modern nation states
teaching us how to draw borders
and build walls
to keep out
what will not be acknowledged
within

187 Andreotti, Stein, and Susa, "From the House That Modernity Built to Healthy Mycelium."

The roof
over our heads
consists of global capital
held together by shareholder financial capitalism
that carries traces of industrial capitalism and state socialism
teaching us in the church of progress, holy capital, and limitless
growth

Looking closely
you can see that this house is not well[188]
When you run your fingers over the walls
you can follow the cracks that start from the bottom
spreading upwards like trees
You find damp roses of discolouration on the ceiling
the air is hard to breathe
and there is a strange smell

You go down to the cellar
to see the plumbing is extracting oil from the ground
and dumping the waste in the backyard
Water comes in clean
and goes out polluted

This house stands on a foundation of separation
from the Earth
and from all living things that together makes Gaia
It teaches us to separate ourselves from the natural world
and to sort and catalogue each other into hierarchies

This foundation of separation
installs fears in us
Fear of change
of scarcity,
worthlessness,
destitution,

188 Andreotti, Stein, and Susa, 3.

existential emptiness,
loss, pain, and death

It shakes us with fear of
impermanence,
incompetence,
and insignificance[189]

So, we compensate
by developing a desire for
accumulation,
for mastery and certainty,
for consensus, coherence
and control

These desires become naturalized
entitlements
that calibrate our hopes and fantasies[190]

This house limits how we think
it limits our imagination[191]

LET GO

Our systems are not resilient to the intrusion of Gaia
eventually they will start to fail
What will we do when the power goes out?
When there is no heating in our house
when we are missing food on our table
and medicine for our kids
There will be war
and we will have to decide whether to stay or go

189 Andreotti, Stein, and Susa, 5.
190 Andreotti, Stein, and Susa, 5.
191 "The house conditions our possibilities for experiencing the world by reducing being to knowing and life to meaning-making" Andreotti, Stein, and Susa, 4.

Gaia's intrusion is unstoppable
we feel it accelerating with every turn of this globe
She is deaf to our pleas for mercy
ignorant of our efforts to make things right
She does not care who is responsible
she is not just
she is not fair
She will not take the role as the righter of wrongs[192]
Gaia does not acknowledge our systems of life,
our money, our Gods, our ethics, our politics
our attempts at love

So, we allow for grief
to break open our hearts
to the inequality of loss
to the unbearable unfairness
that is built into our systems
As power breaks it will show itself
in its most bare and brutal form
there will be no looking away from the houses that we've built
and how they have corrupted us

We will need to let go of our house
We will need to let go of our desire for control and mastery
We will need to let go of defences
of our search for solutions to protect this way of life
We will have to find shelter elsewhere

Let go of any attempt to draw a straight line
from what you already know into the future
there are no linear predictions to be made
that would be too optimistic
Do not underestimate how fast and in what scale this change will
take form[193]

---

192 Stengers, *In Catastrophic Times: Resisting the Coming Barbarism*, 46.
193 Bendell, "Deep Adaptation: A Map for Navigating Climate Tragedy."

Recognize the limits of your knowledge
the restrictions of your experience
the failure of reason in face of catastrophe

Every knowledge is also an ignorance[194]
so you shift your attention
from knowing to learning
to a study of the unknown
a state of deep adaptation

We train for a state of readiness
Here, present and ready

THE UNKNOWN

Gaia asks nothing of us,
she demands nothing.
Her silence is unsettling,
she makes us unsure of how to respond.
How can we answer when there is no question?

The intrusion of Gaia puts a major unknown at the heart of our lives.
This unknown cannot be overcome,
it is not a temporary hurdle or an abyss to cross,
it is here to stay.
The unknown is not a problem to be solved
or a moment that will pass.
We will have to live, in all the ways we can,
with this intrusion to our lives.

Gaia came with a gift that was also a burden. A surprise.[195]
How can we grasp the unknown she has placed with us?

194 de Oliveira (Andreotti), "Education, Knowledge and the Righting of Wrongs," 23.
195 Anderson, "Preemption, Precaution, Preparedness: Anticipatory Action and Future Geographies," 6.

Try to hold it, lightly.
Can you place it between your fingertips?
Do your arms fit around it?
Can you lean on it, like a tree or a big rock?
Can you sense it as a drop of water on your upper lip?
What weight does it hold?

How does it move?
Do you feel a vibration from its core?
Can you sense it pulsating? Does it hold a rhythm?
Does it move with the tempo of eternity, a slow river, a light breeze?
Does it turn around itself? A baby turning in the stomach of their mother, a pebble rolling as a wave hits the shore?

Does it attract everything around it, like a black hole threatening to swallow us?
Or is it an expansive universe, ready to explode?

Listen to this being. Sense its presence.
Let it take form in your mind.

Take a moment to leave the page
let your breath touch your heart and your mind drift
shut your eyes
observe the pictures
screened on the inside of your eyelids

Welcome back
Put your hand on your heart

LIVING ON TOGETHER

How do we live with this unknown at the heart of our lives?
How do we account for this strange presence?
How do we accept that it will impact our lives in unforeseen ways?

Living with the unknown close to heart
means no knowledge has privilege over the other
there is no expertise
no one person has the proper answers
We will have to resist the temptation
to offer hasty solutions
We will have to resist the temptation to separate
and sort according to learnt systems of categorization
not to trust familiar methodologies
and the material we are used to thinking with[196]

Instead, we take care of our doubts
and allow ourselves to hesitate
to be wary
to stammer
and pay attention to what makes us think

We look for connections
and for questions that cannot be appropriated
We find common causes to gather around
in careful collectivity
thinking together as a work to be done[197]

Becoming-with others is how we render each other capable[198]
We are never alone
there is no moving forward by ourselves
We find room to respond

196 Haraway, *Staying with the Trouble: Making Kin in the Chthulucene*. ch. 2.
197 Stengers, *In Catastrophic Times: Resisting the Coming Barbarism*, 132.
198 Haraway, *Staying with the Trouble: Making Kin in the Chthulucene*, 12.

in a multitude of voices
to what initiated Gaia's intrusions
and the consequences of it

There is a strange joy in the presence of catastrophe
that we get to spend time with what's truly important to us
while still holding it lightly[199]

We enter the portal with an awareness
of what we want to let go
and what we want to keep

This future unknown carries no promise
But it offers us work to do
We study for the unknown
We engage without guarantees
We practice our skills of deep adaptation
we respond with all our senses
our full bodies
attending to the movement of this moment
the joy of the first step, even if it is uneasy[200]

Take a breath

Say hello to your feet
your ankles, knees, thighs
your sharp seat bones and your soft ass

Say hello to the small of your back
your lovely stomach
your chest, your breasts
your shoulders, your neck

---

199 Ghadiali, "E45 - Jem Bendell on Deep Adaptation, Climate Change and Societal Collapse // Acceptance and Evolution in the Face of Global Meltdown."

200 Stengers, *In Catastrophic Times: Resisting the Coming Barbarism*, 156.

Say hello to your brilliant head
your upper arms
lower arms
hands and fingers

Look up
Find a horizon
Find people to connect with

BIBLIOGRAPHY

Alexander, M. Jacqui. *Pedagogies of Crossing: Meditations on Feminism, Sexual Politics, Memory and the Sacred.* Durham and London: Duke University Press, 2005.

Anderson, Ben. "Preemption, Precaution, Preparedness: Anticipatory Action and Future Geographies." *Progress in Human Geography,* 2010.

Anderson, Jane. "Negotiating Who 'Owns' Penobscot Culture." *Anthropological Quarterly* 91, no. 1 (2018): 267–305.

Andreotti, Vanessa de Oliveira. "Spivak: Overview of Critique and Educational Propositions (Bergamo)."Accessed September 26, 2018. https://www.academia.edu/4777864/Spivak_overview_of_critique_and_educational_propositions_Bergamo_.

Andreotti, Vanessa, Sharon Stein, and Rene Susa. "From the House That Modernity Built to Healthy Mycelium." *Decolonial Futures Collective*, 02072018. decolonialfutures.net.

Anzaldúa, Gloria. *Borderlands/La Frontera: The New Mestiza.* 4th edition. San Francisco, CA: Aunt Lute Books, 1987.

Barnett, Roland. "Learning for an Unknown Future." *Higher Education Research & Development* 23, no. 3 (2004).

Bendell, Jem. "Deep Adaptation: A Map for Navigating Climate Tragedy." *IFLAS Occasional Paper* 2, July 2018. http://lifeworth.com/deepadaptation.pdf.

Biesta, Gert. "Don't Be Fooled by Ignorant Schoolmasters: On the Role of the Teacher in Emancipatory Education." *Policy Futures in Education* 15, no. 1 (January 1, 2017): 52–73. *The Rediscovery of Teaching.* New York, NY and Oxon: Routledge, 2017.

Bloch, Ernst. *The Principle of Hope Volume I.* Cambridge, Massachusetts: MIT Press, 1953.

Castoriadis, Cornelius. *The Castoriadis Reader / Cornelius Castoriadis. Translated and Edited by David Ames Curtis.* Oxford, UK. Malden, USA.: Blackwell Publishers Ltd, 1997.

Cooper, Susan. *The Dark Is Rising Sequence.* Margret K. McElderry Books, 2013.

Du Bois, W.E.B. *The Souls of Black Folk.* Oxford World's Classics. Oxford: Oxford University Press, 2007.

Duncombe, Stephen. *Thomas More Open Utopia.* Minor Compositions, 2012.

Ellsworth, Elizabeth. "Why Doesn't This Feel Empowering? Working Through the Repressive Myths of Critical Pedagogy." *Harvard Educational Review* 59, no. 3 (1989): 297–324.

Erickson, Milton H. "Pediatric Hypnotherapy." *The American Journal of Clinical Hypnosis, Reprinted in Collected Papers Vol.4,* 1958.

Erickson, Milton H, and Ernest L Rossi. "Two-Level Communication and the Microdynamics of Trance and Suggestion." *The American Journal of Clinical Hypnosis, Reprinted in Collected Papers Vol.1,* 1976.

"Exploring the Animal Turn." Accessed October 11, 2021. https://www.pi.lu.se/en/publications/pufendorf-ias-publications/exploring-animal-turn.

Freire, Paulo. *Education for Critical Consciousness.* London. New York.: Continuum, 1974.
———.*Pedagogy of Freedom – Ethics, Democracy, and Civic Courage.*

Lanham: Rowman & Littlefield Publishers, 2000.

———.*Pedagogy of the Oppressed.* London: Penguin Books, 1970.

Gershon, Walter S. "Double Binds, Ab-Uses, and a Hopeless Hope: Epistemological Possibilities and Sensual Questions for Spivak's Introductory Framing of An Aesthetic Education in the Era of Globalization." Critical Literacy: Theories and Practices 9, no. 1 (2015).

Ghadiali, Amisha. "E45 – Jem Bendell on Deep Adaptation, Climate Change and Societal Collapse // Acceptance and Evolution in the Face of Global Meltdown." Accessed May 19, 2020. https://www.thefutureisbeautiful.co/2018/12/27/e45-jem-bendell-on-deep-adaptation-climate-change-and-societal-collapse-acceptance-and-evolution-in-the-face-of-global-meltdown/.

Gillen, Jay. *Educating for Insurgency: The Roles of Young People in Schools of Poverty.* Oakland: AK Press, 2014.

Greenwood, Susan. "The Owl, the Dragon and the Magician: Reflections on Being an Anthropologist Studying Magic."*The Pomegranate Special Issue* Vol 17, no. 1–2 (2016): 141–54.

Haraway, Donna. *Staying with the Trouble: Making Kin in the Chthulucene.* Durham and London: Duke University Press, 2016.

Hardy, Karl. "Unsettling Hope: Contemporary Indigenous Politics, Settler-Colonialism, and Utopianism." *Spaces of Utopia: An Electronic Journal* 2, no. 1 (2012): 123–36.

Harney, Stefano, and Fred Moten. *The Undercommons: Fugitive Planning & Black Study.* Wivenhoe: Minor Compositions, 2013.

Heli, Susanna. *Föda Utan Rädsla.* Stockholm: Bonnier Existens, 2009.

Hill Collins, Patricia. *Black Feminist Thought: Knowledge, Consciousness, and the Politics of Empowerment.* New York, NY: Psychology Press, 2000.

hooks, bell. *Talking Back - Thinking Feminist, Thinking Black.* Vol. 2. Boston: South End Press, 1989.

———.*Teaching Community: A Pedagogy of Hope.* New York,NY: Routledge, 2003.

———.*Teaching to Transgress: Education as the Practice of Freedom.* New York,NY: Routledge, 1994.

"Insight Timer – #1 Free Meditation App for Sleep, Relax & More." Accessed October 11, 2021. https://insighttimer.com/.

Kapoor, Ilan. "Hyper-Self-Reflexive Development? Spivak on Representing the Third World'Other'." *Third World Quarterly* 25, no. 4 (2004): 627–47.

Levitas, Ruth. "Looking for the Blue: The Necessity of Utopia." *Journal of Political Ideologies* 12:3 (2007): 289–306.
Lorde, Audre. Sister Outsider. New York, NY: Random House Inc., 1984.

Martinez, Theresa A. "The Double-Consciousness of Du Bois & The 'Mestiza Consciousness' of Anzaldúa." *Race, Gender & Class Vol.9, no. 4 (2002): 158–76.*

Milder, Patricia. "TEACHING AS ART The Contemporary Lecture-Performance." *PAJ: A Journal of Performance and Art* 1, no. 33 (2010): 13–27.

Minh-ha, Trinh T. Woman, Native, Other. Writing Postcoloniality and Feminism. Bloomington and Indianapolis: Indiana University Press, 1989.

Monti, Adriana. *Scuola Senza Fine*, 1983. http://www.universitadelledonne.it/english/scuola%20senza%20fine.htm.

Ng, Roxana. "Decolonizing Teaching and Learning Through Embodied Learning: Toward an Integrated Approach." In *Sharing Breath Embodied Learning and Decolonization*, edited by Sheila Batacharya and Yuk-Lin Renita Wong. Edmonton, AU: AU Press, 2018.

Nyberg, Lisa. "INDUCTION: An Unknown at the Heart of Our Lives." *Periskop: Forum for Kunsthistorisk Debat*, no. 24 (2020): 48–61.

Nyberg, Lisa, and Johanna Gustavsson. "Radikal Pedagogik." Accessed March 6, 2017. http://radikalpedagogik.blogspot.com/. Oliveira (Andreotti), Vanessa de. "Education, Knowledge and the Righting of Wrongs." *Other Education: The Journal of Educational Alternatives* 1, no. 1 (2012): 19–31.

Piercy, Jennifer. "Bone Deep Sleep | Insight Timer." Accessed October 12, 2021. https://insighttimer.com/jenniferpiercy/guided-meditations/bone-deep-sleep.

Podesva, Kristina Lee. "A Pedagogical Turn: Brief Notes on Education as Art." Fillip, 2007. https://fillip.ca/content/a-pedagogical-turn.

Rancière, Jacques. *The Ignorant Schoolmaster, Five Lessons in Intellectual Emancipation*. Stanford, California: Stanford University Press, 1991.

———. **"Un-What?"** In *The Pedagogics of Unlearning*, 25–46. Earth, Milky Way: punctum books, 2016.

Rosen, Sidney. *My Voice Will Go with You: The Teaching Tales of Milton H. Erickson*. New York,NY and London,UK: W.W. Norton and Company, Inc., 1991.

Rossi, Ernest L. *The Nature of Hypnosis and Suggestion. The Collected Papers of Milton H. Erickson on Hypnosis, Volume 1.* New York, NY: Halsted Press, 1980.

Sandoval, Chela. *Methodology of the Oppressed.* Minneapolis: University of Minnesota Press, 2000.

Scheper-Hughes, Nancy. "A Finger in the Wound: On Pain, Scars, and Suffering." *Representations* 146, no. 1 (2019): 32–58.

Shklovsky, Viktor. "Art as Device." In *Theory Of Prose.* London: Kalkey Archive Press, 1991.

Solnit, Rebecca. *Hope in the Dark: Untold Histories Wild Possibilities.* Edinburgh: Canongate Books, 2016.

Spivak, Gayatri Chakravorty. *An Aesthetic Education in the Era of Globalization.* Cambridge, Massachusetts: Harvard University Press, 2012.

———.*The Post-Colonial Critic: Interviews, Strategies, Dialogues.* New York, NY: Routledge, 1990.

Stengers, Isabelle. *In Catastrophic Times: Resisting the Coming Barbarism.* Lüneburg: Open Humanities Press, meson press, 2015.

Veracini, Lorenzo. "Introducing Settler Colonial Studies." *Settler Colonial Studies* 1, no. 1 (2011): 1–12.

———.**The Settler Colonial Present.** Springer, 2015.

Webber, John, and RJ Thomas. "Talking Therapy Ep. 28 Dr. Jeffrey Zeig on the Evolution of Psychotherapy." Accessed December 5, 2019. http://www.talkingtherapypodcast.com/.

DOCUMENTATION

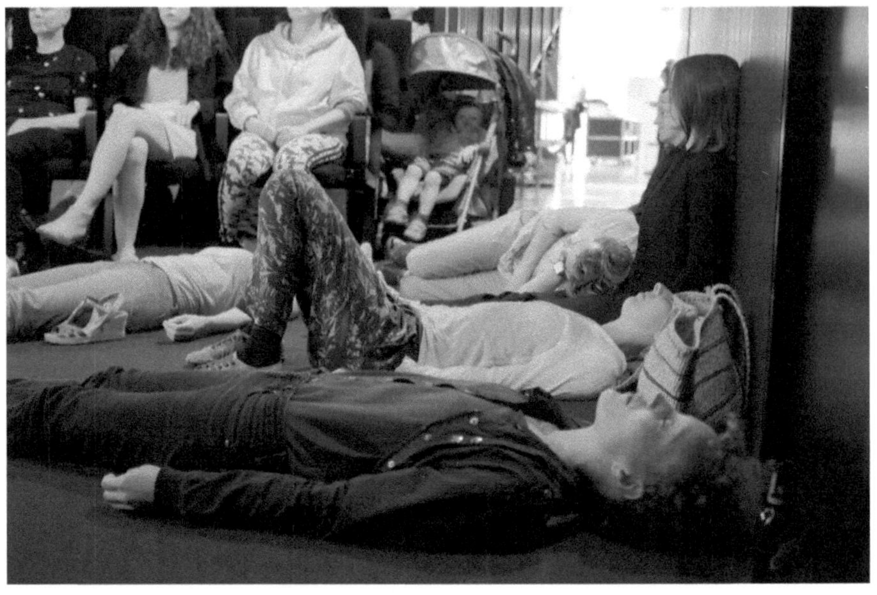

Photo: Keiko Uenishi

ENTER/EXIT – A GUIDED MEDITATION TO THE POINT OF NO RETURN

Performance (live voice, recorded soundtrack), 15 minutes
During the event HAUNTOPIA/What If at MUMOK, Vienna
June 8th 2016

Summary

THE MEDITATION IS CENTERED AROUND A STORY of the protagonist arriving in Europe, Vienna, making the walk from the subway station to the MUMOK museum and down to the room where the real life event takes place. The protagonist is carrying a stone in their pocket that needs to be hidden and concealed.

The surroundings are described in a way that makes them a bit alien or strange, as if the protagonist is new to the place. At the same time, they recognize themselves as part of the cultural crowd that belongs to this kind of place. The protagonist is constantly reassured that they will fit in and not be noticed, that they are okay.

In the end the protagonist takes out the stone and releases its hidden powers.

Manuscript

Find a place to sit or lay down, comfortably. Take off your shoes if you like. Take a deep breath, in (breath) and out (breath). Once more, in (breath) and out (breath). And on your third breath (breath) when you breathe out, let your eyes close (breath).

Keep breathing, as you normally would, without effort.
Notice your breathing; air rushing into your nostrils,
into all the cavities in your head,
down your throat to your lungs and stomach.
Feel your chest expand for every breath,
and decline as the air is gently pushed out.
Feel your body resting against the chair or the ground.
You are supported.
Let your shoulders relax, your arms, hands, backside, legs, feet.
Let your face relax.

Here you are.
How did you get here?
At some point you came, and you were received.
Your feet landed on the ground. You arrived.
You came to Europe, remember?
Maybe you were born here.
Maybe you travelled. Maybe you were forced to.
Maybe someone carried you close to their body.
Maybe you longed to come.
You came to Vienna. Maybe you spent your childhood in these streets.
Maybe you flew here on the cheapest ticket with headphones to escape some of the noise.
Maybe love brought you.
Anyway, you are here now.

You are standing in a moving escalator, your right hand resting on the hand rail. Slowly the stairs are lifting you, up, up, up towards the light. You exit the stairs and step out into the street. You are standing between tall white buildings, exquisitely embellished facades, tall windows, marble statues looking down from rooftops, neat gardens with form cut trees and pathways. In the air a light, sweet smell of flowers, greens, dust and warm asphalt. For a moment you have the distinct feeling of time travel, an alien experience, is this really now, is this really real?

Your hand goes to your jacket, to your left pocket for reassurance. Through the fabric you can feel a hard object. You reach into the pocket and with your fingertips you can feel a stone; small, round and smooth, cool to the touch. You turn it between your fingers until you find the place where a piece is shipped off; a ragged surface, a sharp edge. You press it against your index finger. The feeling is very familiar. You realize you've been holding your breath for a moment, but now you let the air out (breath).

The sound of traffic brings you back, and reminds you to keep to the sidewalk. A cream coloured wall is stretching out on your left side. You start walking, following the wall. You are looking for a place to enter, an opening. The sunlight is reflecting from the wall, making the sidewalk bright and warm. Big signs get your attention and point you in the right direction. This is the main entrance. Three arches divided by pillars. You turn your back to the traffic and choose to enter through the middle archway. Somehow it seems appropriate.

On the other side of the wall, the space opens up to a big square the size of a football field. The square is flanked on each side by two huge cubes. To your left is a white cube, big as a six-storey building. To you right an equally big cube in dark grey. Stone cubes. They seem like enclosed objects, resting heavy on the ground. Stairs that are leading up to a tiny entrance reveal that they are actually buildings.

You are not surprised. These are aesthetically bold choices. You might not like them, but you recognize them as such and the cultural capital that comes with this architecture. You are not intimidated. You might have been at some point, but not anymore. You know that you are granted access. You have come so far.

You take a deep breath, and head for the dark, grey building, crossing the square. It is crowded with people sitting in clusters; paying customers by tables with coffees and wine glasses, students and backpackers lingering on the colourful, playful formations that serve as benches. Light clothes, heavy bags, phones in hand. You can distinguish between tourists and cultural workers as yourself. Those who visit, those who belong; you all have access.

You have done what needs to be done. Maybe you have straightened your hair and put a new shirt on. Maybe you wear black, neat pieces, accessorised with a contrasting colour. Maybe your shoes are fancy and if not, they are okay. You are okay. No one will ask you to leave. No one can tell what is in your pocket.

You ascend the stairs to the building. Up close the grey stone gives up an unexpected smell of rivers, sand beds, caves. A hint of the earth they were excavated from. The entrance is in shadows, wide and low, as if pressed down by the weight of the building. Even though the doors are made of glass, the shade makes them opaque and you cannot see what is on the other side. Still, you push through. You are invited.

Inside the air is cool, comfortable, tempered. The walls are made of the same dark stone as the facade, as if the rooms have been carefully carved out of a solid block. The effect is massive. You feel both intimidated and impressed. This is an institution that does not deny its powers. Your heart feels suddenly compressed by the weight, a pressure that spreads over your chest, up to your throat, out like a tingling feeling in your arms.

You take a deep breath (breath) and listen to your heart.
It is still beating.
The pressure fades for each breath. Good.

You take a look around. To your right, glass walls are revealing an exhibition of smaller paintings and sculptures of European post-war modernism. To your left is a white space with square, symmetric shelves, carefully stacked with books, lamps and other objects in perfect formation and bright lighting. There is a big counter with a woman in proper, black clothing.

Straight ahead are the elevators, glass cubes in wires going up and down an open shaft. Between you and the elevators is a square hole in the floor, protected by a glass fence. You put your hands on the cool glass and look down. You can see all the way down to the bottom floor, some 12 meters down. Vertigo makes you clasp to the glass. Looking up you see even further, you count to four floors and a glass ceiling, a square glimpse of the blue sky above, visible through a tunnel of massive stone.

You need to get to the bottom floor, so you go up to the woman at the counter. You do your best to muster a smile that will appear friendly, but not too eager. Unsuspicious, safe. Your left arm pushes towards your body, blocking the pocket of your jacket. She greets you with a short welcome, and you tell her you want to visit the event in the kino. You swipe your card, push the code and get a ticket. You thank her and head towards the elevators. That was easy. You are still smiling.

Just when you're about to reach the elevators, someone calls your attention: "Excuse me". You stare at the young woman. You can feel the tingling of sweat breaking out on your forehead, what is wrong? "Your ticket please." Ah, the ticket, it is still in your hand. You hand it over and step towards the elevator doors. No one is calling you back. You push the button and glance back at the young woman. She is already occupied with other visitors. You step into the elevator and push to go down. As the elevator descends your hands go to your face, your fingers on each side of the nose, stroking your cheeks, your chin, as if wiping the smile off your face. You let out a big yawn (yawn) and your body feels more relaxed. You are so close now.

With a "ping" the elevator doors open, and you step out into an empty room, with an open door at the end. You can hear the sounds of people, socialising and talking. As you come closer you recognize bits of conversations, in German and English, light laughter, fabrics rubbing against fabrics, soft music in the background. It is bright though there are no windows, the walls are white. You head towards the bar, but before you get to it, the music stops and you are all instructed to head towards the screening room to the left, and find a comfortable place to sit or lie down. You follow the crowd into the dark room, then hesitate a bit until people start to settle down. You find a place where you feel safe.

A voice instructs you to sit as comfortable as possible, to take a deep breath in, and out (breath) and to close your eyes. You look around and wait, until everyone has closed theirs before you close your own. The voice continues, but you are not listening anymore. Your hand goes to your pocket, to the cool, round object. Carefully you pull it out and keep it hidden in your hand.

You have arrived.
This is it.
There will be no turning back.
Nothing will ever be the same.
All you know will be unlearned.
All the truths will come untrue.
A wind will blow. A rain will come.
Subatomic particles will collide and start a chain reaction.
The earth will move.
Dark, grey stone will turn to sand.
What you thought mattered will not matter anymore.

In your hand the stone has adapted to your body's temperature.
You feel completely calm. Your breathing is soft. Your hands are still.
It is time.
You open your hand and release the stone.

Thank you.
Please take a moment to awaken your body. Move your fingers and hands, toes and feet.
Open your eyes. Blink. Have a look around, remind yourself of where you are.
Thank you for participating.

Photo: Lisa Nyberg

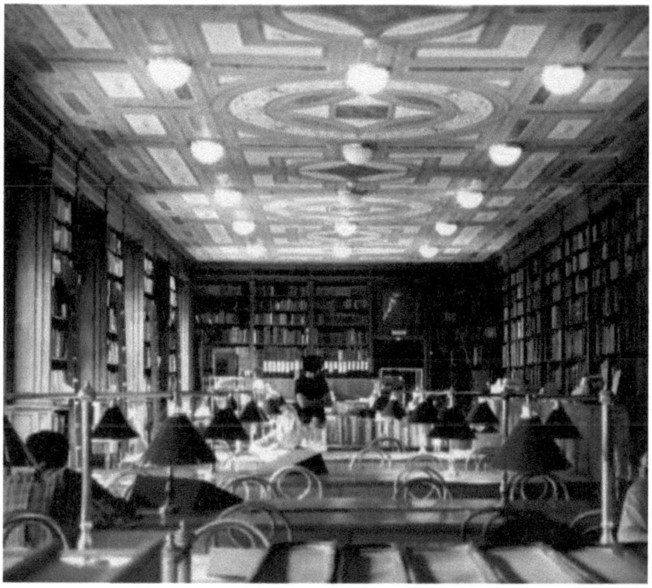

UNSETTLING I: SCHILLERPLATZ

Sound piece for headphones, 15.50 minutes
Presented at Rundgang, Akademie der bildenden Künste, Vienna, 2017
Voice: Lisa Nyberg
Sound: A sound clip of the string quartet Felberer Streich playing the piece Am Schillerplatz, has been stretched digitally, from 30 seconds to 15 minutes.

Listen at https://soundcloud.com/elmkbkwbciyu/unsettelingischiller-platz/s-QJMIy

Summary
This guided meditation invites you to tune in to the rhythm of your body, and to be aware of your pulsating presence and the impact you have on your surroundings. Gradually, the focus shifts to the interface between you and your surroundings and to the other souls of the house. These souls interrupt your rhythm with dissonance and demand your attention.

Manuscript

Hi. Welcome.

This is a guided meditation for headphones, produced specifically for the Rundgang exhibition of 2017 at the Academy of Fine Arts, Vienna. It is recorded by me, Lisa Nyberg, as part of the program of HAUNTOPIA, put together by the candidates of the PhD-in-Practice program. For more information, please visit the website.

Now, the meditation is meant to be listened to in the Art Academy's building at Schillerplatz in central Vienna. Find a place where you can have some peace and will not be disturbed. You can still choose a crowded room, but find a corner, and signal to other people that you are occupied. You can sit or stand, but this meditation is not suitable for laying down. The meditation is about 15 minutes long.

Make sure your headphones fit alright, and that you can find a position that is relaxing and comfortable. Please pause the recording until you have found such a place.

Are you ready? Here we go.

Please relax. Feet firmly on the floor, an even distribution of weight between your left and right, a straight back. Take a deep breath, and let your shoulders down. One more – and out. Once more, and close your eyes. You can also keep them fixated on one spot on the floor or wall in front of you.

Keep on breathing, as you normally would, without effort.

This exercise starts with listening, with your whole body. From the inside-out. Listen to your body, listen for a rhythm. Your body, as any body with a pulse, is never really still. There is always movement; small shifts of weight from one side to the other, muscles tensing up or relaxing, a constant balancing act to keep your body upright. The movement of your chest when you breathe, affecting your whole torso to expand and retract. You can feel a tingling on the top of your head; your hair is growing, your nails are growing, your skin is renewing itself from the inside; cells shifting places, from inside to out, until they reach the surface and let go, in the shredding of skin and hair. Everywhere you go you're leaving a dusty trace behind you. Feel the vibration of inter-cellular motion, electrons circulating the nucleus, atoms bouncing off atoms, cells dividing and multiplying. The ongoing life and death, building up and breaking down, of your body.

Your body is making a symphony that follows the score laid out by your DNA. There is a system, a plan, a map for all this activity. A turning motion of rotating steps. A life making, pulsating rhythm. It all comes together in a crescendo of blood rushing through veins, your heart pumping in a steady, galloping bo-bo-bom, bo-bo-bom, bo-bo-bom, oxygen pulsating out through your limbs. Food being pushed through your intestines by muscles squeezing in perfect formation. In your mouth, underneath your tongue, a small pool of saliva is being constantly refilled before it overflows – and you swallow.

Can you feel it all moving? Building up, breaking down, dividing, coming together, multiplying, letting go... Like waves crashing on a shore. There is a rhythm in this chaos. You can feel it, you can follow it. You are made of this rhythm. It is at the centre of you. Feel it in your stomach, in your liver, your kidneys, your intestines. Let it bounce between your hip bones. Let it pulsate in your sex.

Take a deep breath – in, out – and hold the rhythm in your mind. Focus the rhythm to your feet. Let them go with it, let them move. The response can be small or big, visible on barely noticeable. Shift the focus to your hands, bringing the rhythm to your fingers and thumbs. Move it up to your neck and shoulders. Now, let the rhythm rest in whatever part of your body that feels natural. It is just there. It is yours.

Your never-ending movement produces heat. This is one of the things that make you attractive to others. The heat shows on your skin; how it is constantly shifting in colour, darkens when blood rushes to cheeks and ears and chest. Heat radiates from you, bringing with it small particles from your body, smells of perspiration, of your skin, of your mucus, of your blood. You are alive, a lively pulsating presence. This is the impact you have on your surroundings. When you enter a room you bring movement, vibrations, heat, smells, small particles of yourself as a trace of your presence.

You are magnetic. Energies are pulsating in circular loops from your head to your toes, expanding from your every movement, throwing a net of magnetic fields that attract and repel your surroundings in a pulsating traction. Other bodies are drawn to you, caught in your pulsating web of energies.

Now, I need you to reach through your self-centred presence. Try to focus on the interface between your body and the surroundings. Your skin. The small hairs on your cheeks and chin and arms, registering and reacting to the temperature around you. The tip of your nose, air flowing in and out of your body. Where you end and something, someone, else begins is not totally clear. In the interface you and other mix at the border. In the air you breathe. In the light breeze that touches your forearm. Now.

You are not alone. Can you sense them?
This building is inhabited by a lot more beings than the human living. Many souls have passed through this house, differently affected, bringing something with them, leaving something else behind. But some stay. They just won't leave. They walk these corridors. They have been crying in these stairs. They have been hiding in the shadows in the basement. They have been sitting where you are sitting now. They roam around the building, mixing in with the shadows or the light. Too close or too far away, they are out of focus. They are being unreasonable.

You need to let go of reason. You have ignored other forms of presence, other time-space beings. Your logic is in the way, you have cut off connections, you are not listening. They are here, all the time.

They are not over there, overseas, underground, on the other side, in another time or dimension. They are connected with you and they will not be contained or repressed. They are laying a hand on your shoulder. Listen. They tell you they have been wronged. Their case is unsolved. They are not ready to move on. They have not been heard. They play at the end of your audible sound spectrum, too high or too low, listen for a shriek or a murmur.

Their rhythm is nothing like yours. It is not in harmony, it is dissonant, going and stopping in unforeseeable intervals. They refuse to fall into rhythm, to mix in with the dominant score. To you, it sounds like things falling, crashing, scraping, breaking. In the corner of your eye, they are a blur, a shimmer, a flash of light. You feel them as a light touch, a reoccurring itch, a sense of chill at the back of your neck, or a sudden heat of someone next to you. They demand your attention. They are a disturbance. An interruption.

Let yourself be interrupted.

Let your inner rhythm be upset, upset by another rhythm. Take it in. Let it happen.
Lend yourself to a radical openness. You do not need to resist. You do not want to. You wanted something to change, something radical. Here is your chance.
Feel your body start to shake. Your rhythm is colliding and bouncing off another rhythm.
Your knees, your thighs, your shoulders. Let yourself be shaken. Over-taken.
Let go of control. Shake the walls of reality until all is a blur. You are breaking up.
You are de-connecting, re-connecting.
Something over-and-done with will come back to you. The unfamiliar will come into view.
Your blind spot will re-focus. You will see outside of yourself.
You need to start moving. Something needs to be done. It is in your hands. It is in you. It is on you. Go.
Go.
Go.

Thank you. Please take a moment to come back. Move your fingers, and hands, toes and feet. Open your eyes. Blink. Have a look around, remind yourself of where you are.

Thank you for participating.

Photo: Lisa Nyberg

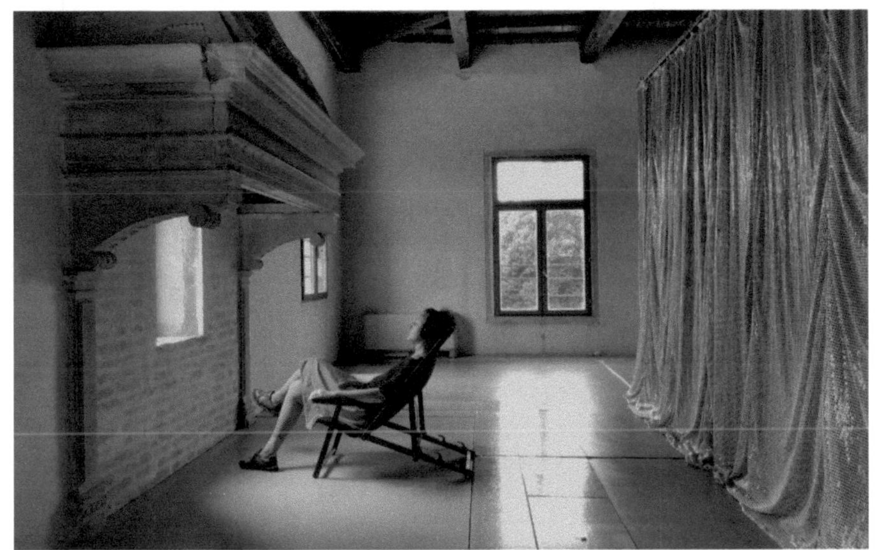

UNSETTLING II: A GUIDED MEDITATION TO THE SEA

Sound installation, 18 minutes
HAUNTOPIA/What if exhibition at the Research Pavilion in Venice, 2017
Text and voice: Lisa Nyberg
Sound and mixing: Julia Giertz
Soundbox: Terje Östling
Available at
https://soundcloud.com/elmkbkwbciyu/unsettlingii-a-guided-meditation-to-the-sea/s-bFEXR

Summary
The work deals with unsettling and de-centering by the means of meditation. A voice guides the listener through an awareness exercise, where one's body is soaked into the sea, and the rhythm of one's body is disrupted by a call from the deep. There is an element of "soft cohesion", a persuasiveness of the voice, guiding the listener to dispossess of the current reality, falling into another rhythm, to be possessed and unsettled. In the process there is also space for negotiation and resistance.

Manuscript

in

I welcome you to this guided meditation to the sea. This journey will take about 18 minutes.

During this time, you might experience some discomfort. That is okay. As the title suggests, this meditation can be an unsettling experience. I invite you to take the risk.

If you at any time feel like you do not want to continue, simply open your eyes and remove the headphones.

You are welcome to start over at any time. Please have a seat, settle down. Find a way to increase your level
of comfort. Take off your shoes if you like, your jacket. Have some water.

1.

Here we go
Relax into the chair
Feel how it supports you
It is there for you
Trust that you are safe in this moment
You are allowed a break
from walking
from looking
from talking and smiling
from attentiveness to other people
Close your eyes
calling back
all of the energies,
all the attention to outer stimulation
Bring it back
into your body
You are here
Simply between earth and sky
Together
we are here with you
Take a deep breath

in...
and out....
Breathing out tensions
Let your shoulders down
One more in...
down your stomach
and out....
Relaxing all the little muscles around the eyes
Letting go of face
mask
expressions
Keep on breathing, as you normally would
without effort
Let your jaw drop
opening a pathway
between inner
and outer
you
Feel your breath
coming and going
endlessly
Feel your body space
expand
and retract
Your breath
like waves
rocking your body
back and forth like a baby
Let yourself be comforted
by the steady rhythm
of automatic breathing
With every breath
you let go of
thinking
rationalizing
efficiency

progress
to give room for sensing
feeling
being
and making contact

2.
Tune in to the space around you
space above you
space to the left
space to the right
space beneath you
The chair is connected to the floor
Feel the space between the chair and the floor
The floor is connected to the building
Feel the space between the walls of the building, between floor and ceiling
The building is connected to the ground
Feel the vastness of Earth beneath you
the ground connected to the ocean
the deep
Let your body
dissolve
into the sea
The small holes in your skin
soaking up the salty water
by capillary power
There is nothing you need to do
Just let it happen
Feel your body getting heavier
and heavier
until you go in
to go under
Notice the water's surface in front of you
a shiny, glimmering surface

reflecting what is above
opaque to what is beneath
Feel it passing by your face
your chin
your mouth
your nose
your eyes
your forehead
until you see the surface shimmering from beneath
Light above you
dark beneath you
Falling slowly
down
and dark
Know yourself
in this deep dark place
in this state of falling
of letting go
of giving in

3.
Now it is time
to assimilate to the environment
and adapt our breathing to the ocean
You came from water, remember?
Your body is adaptable
you are prone to change
You can live in water
you did so for months
you just need to remind yourself
We're going to take a deep breath together
with force
breathing liquid into our lungs
3, 2, 1 and
(in)
Let the water pass your lips, your mouth, your throat,

down your lungs
take it in (in)
Feel the taste of salt, tearing at your throat
the burn that hits your lungs
Let it burn
This burn will sustain you
You will live in this pain
We are together in this pain
This is the necessary connection
of living body to body
Water in, water out
Suffering is essential
just hold on
Keep on breathing
one breath at a time
Focus on the rhythm
of natural breath
It will keep you alive
You are breathing water
We are breathing water
Water is life
Water is life

4.
Open your ears
to a sound
Follow the sound emerging from the deep
from the abyss beneath you
At first it's just a single note
Listen to this note in your head
The note starts to pulsate
into a rhythm
Listen to this rhythm
Hold on to it
Hold on to this sound wave

emerging from the depths
Imagine the source of this sound
Imagine the membrane that produces it
The mouth making the sound
this call
What is calling you?
Who is calling you?
What is this presence?

5.
Finally, you land
The natural state of free falling is interrupted
when your feet hit the sandy ocean floor
The sound is now a strong presence
The mouth of the sound is coming near
In front of you
a face is emerging from the dark waters
The face
of the mouth
of the membrane
calling you
Calling your attention from the deep
Meet this face,
no need to hide, to look away
This is the face
a body of water facing you
Concentrate on this presence
Meet this child
this mother
this brother
this lost love
whose mouth is open
forever open
calling you
Listen to the call
Focus on the message
This is important

You will have to remember this message
to bring it with you when you leave

6.
Finally, it is time to go
You bend you knees
and push away from the ocean floor
Rising up towards the surface
the water around you goes from black
to bluer
and bluer
and lighter
until you reach the surface
the light hits your eyelids
and you break through
Getting out of the water
you are heavy
You open your mouth, your throat
to let the water spill out of your lungs
on to the ground and trickle back to sea
Still
the ocean is part of you now
It lingers
in your clothes, your skin, your flesh
How will you carry yourself from the deep?
How will you carry the call
that is still resonating within you
that echoes in your cavities?
Your body is now a carrier of this message
As you walk the ground, your feet will be wet
You will leave marks in your path
of the deep
When you run your tongue over your lips
you will be able to taste the salt
the sea
to remember

what is under the surface
The rhythm
the call
the face
the message
You will know
and you will find a way
to respond
out
It is time to connect again with the outer world.
Slowly wake up your body.
Wiggle your toes, your fingers.
Move your head a little from side to side.
Open your mouth to a big yawn.
Open your eyes. Blink.
Look around, remind yourself of where you are.
Thank you for participating.

Unsettling III: Together to the sea

Performance by Julia Giertz (sound) and Lisa Nyberg (text and voice), approx. 20 minutes
EARN conference HAUNTOPIA/What If at the Research Pavilion in Venice
September 9th 2017

Summary

This performance is an adaptation of the sound installation Unsettling II: A guided meditation to the sea to fit a live performance. The voice addresses a collective as well as the individual, guiding the attention towards the other bodies in the room, to tune in to each other for a sense of taking this journey together. The sound s performed live, merging sampling with synthesizers.

Manuscript

This meditation is part of my research on Pedagogies of the Unknown. From a backdrop of intersectional feminist self-organization and radical pedagogy, this is a step out into the Un-. Uncertainty. Unsettling. Unrest. Guided meditations as a methodology for me comprises many of the tensions and conflicts embedded in the search for a truly radical pedagogy – between cohesion and consent, between relations of power and relations of Eros, love, of trust, negotiations of agency, obstacles, restrictions, resistance, refusal and a radical openness. A version of this meditation can be found in the exhibition, as a sound piece for headphones, but mostly I've been experimenting with guided imagery as live performance, as a lecture or a lesson, as storytelling and related forms of embodied study.

Today's guided meditation is a journey to the depths of the Mediterranean Sea. With this town and its buildings literally resting on its surface, this journey brings a meeting with a rhythm, a sound, a face, a message. I will be your guide, together with Julia Giertz who is the shaper of sounds. This is our first time working together, so we're very excited.

During this time, you might experience some discomfort. That is okay. As the title suggests, this meditation can for some, or somehow, be an unsettling experience. We invite you to take the risk and follow us on this journey.

If you at any time feel like you don't want to continue, simply open your eyes to distance yourself from what is going on; move your body around a bit, you can even check your phone, but please don't take any pictures, and try not to disturb the other participants. Try to enjoy this pocket of rest.

For those of you who have fears related to deep water, who feel like they are in an especially suggestive state today, or just not in the mood, please step out now, before we begin. You can always listen in the exhibition whenever you feel like it.
Find a seat. We prefer if you do not lie down, sitting up better asserts your agency.

in
We welcome you to this guided meditation to the sea. This journey will take about 18 minutes.
During this time, you do not have to sit perfectly still – you are allowed to shift and move around as needed.
Have a seat. Find a way to increase your level of comfort.
Take off your shoes if you like, your jacket. Have some water.

1.
Here we go
Relax into the chair
Feel how it supports you
It is there for you
Trust that you are safe in this moment
You are allowed a break
from walking
from looking
from talking and smiling

from attentiveness to other people
Close your eyes
calling back
all of the energies,
all the attention to outer stimulation
Bring it back
into your body
You are here
Simply between earth and sky
Together
we are here with you
We will take a deep breath
in...
and out....
Breathing out tensions
Let your shoulders down
One more in...
down your stomach
and out....
Relaxing all the little muscles around the eyes
Letting go of face
mask
expressions
Keep on breathing, as you normally would
without effort
Let you jaw drop
opening a pathway
between inner
and outer
you

2.

Tune in to the bodies around you
Bodies in front of you
Bodies to the left
Bodies to the right

Bodies behind you
Feel them breathing
pulsating
radiating heat
Feel your body longing for the others
Falling into a common rhythm
Your senses reaching
through the air
like tentacles of energy
making a thick, human atmosphere
a larger body space
of lungs, limbs, liquids, longings
Being together
Breathing together
Feel your breathing
coming and going
endlessly
Feel your body space
expand
and retract
Your breath
like waves
rocking your body
back and forth like a baby
Let yourself be comforted
by the steady rhythm
of automatic breathing
With every breath
we let go of
thinking
rationalizing
efficiency
progress
to give room for sensing
feeling
being together

and making contact
The chairs we rest on are connected to the building
Feel the floor of the building
connecting to the brick walls
layers upon layers
holding up the ceiling
this container of air
This building stands on a construction of stones and wooden piles
This town rests on a man-made forest
submerged in a still lagoon
Water slowly moving between the tree trunks
fish gathering in their shadow
Feel the vastness of water beneath you
a body of water
a sea
We are going to let our bodies
dissolve
into the sea
The small holes in your skin
soaking up the salty water
by capillary power
There is nothing you need to do
just let it happen
Feel your body getting heavier
and heavier
until you go in
to go under
Notice the water's surface in front of you
a shiny, glimmering surface
reflecting what is above
opaque to what is beneath
Feel it passing by your face
your chin
your mouth
your nose
your eyes

your forehead
until you see the surface shimmering from beneath
Light above you
dark beneath you
Falling slowly
down
and dark
Know yourself
in this deep dark place
in this state of falling
of letting go
of giving in

3.
Now it is time
to assimilate to the environment
and adapt our breathing to the sea
We came from water, remember?
Our bodies are adaptable
We are prone to change
We can live in water
We did so for months
You just need to remind yourself
We're going to take a deep breath
with force
breathing the water into our lungs
3, 2, 1 and
(in)
Let the water pass your lips, your mouth, your throat, down your lungs
Take it in (in)
Taste the salt in your mouth, tearing at your throat
the burn that hits our lungs
Let it burn
This burn will sustain you
We will live in this pain

We are together in this pain
This is the necessary connection
of living body to body
Water in, water out
Suffering is essential
just hold on
Keep on breathing
one breath at a time
Focus on the rhythm
of natural breath
It will keep you alive
You are breathing water
We are breathing water
Water is life
Water is life

4.
Open your ears
to a sound
Follow the sound emerging from the deep
from the abyss beneath you
At first it's just a single note
Listen to this note in your head
The note starts to pulsate
into a rhythm
Listen to this rhythm
Hold on to it
Hold on to this sound wave
emerging from the depths
Imagine the source of this sound
Imagine the membrane that produces it
The mouth making the sound
this call
What is calling us?
Who is calling us?
What is this presence?

5.
Finally, we land
The natural state of free falling is interrupted
by a soft landing
as your feet hit the sandy ocean floor
The sound is now a strong presence
The mouth of the sound is coming near
In front of us
a face is emerging from the dark waters
The face
of the mouth
of the membrane
calling us
calling our attention from the deep
Meet this face,
no need to hide, to look away
This is the face
a body of water facing you
Concentrate on this presence
Meet this child
this mother
this brother
this lost love
whose mouth is open
forever open
calling us
Listen to the call
Focus on the message
This is important
We will have to remember this message
to bring it with us when we leave

6.
Finally, it is time to go
you bend your knees
and push away from the ocean floor
Rising up towards the surface
the water around us goes from black
to bluer
and bluer
and lighter
until we reach the surface
the light hits our eyelids
and we break through
Getting out of the water
we are heavy
You open your mouth, your throat
to let the water spill out of your lungs
on to the ground and trickle back to sea
Still
the ocean is part of us now
it lingers
in our clothes, our skin, our flesh
As we walk the ground your feet will be wet
We will leave marks in our path
of the deep
When you run your tongue over your lips
you will be able to taste the salt
the sea
to remember
what is under the surface
The rhythm
The call
The face
The message
We will know
and we will find a way
to respond
out

It is time to connect again with the outer world.
Slowly wake up your body. Wiggle your toes, your fingers.
Move your head a little from side to side.
You can open your mouth to a big yawn.
Open your eyes, blink. Look around to remind yourself of where you are.
Check that you are okay. Check that the people around you are okay.
Bring each other back to the present.

Thank you.

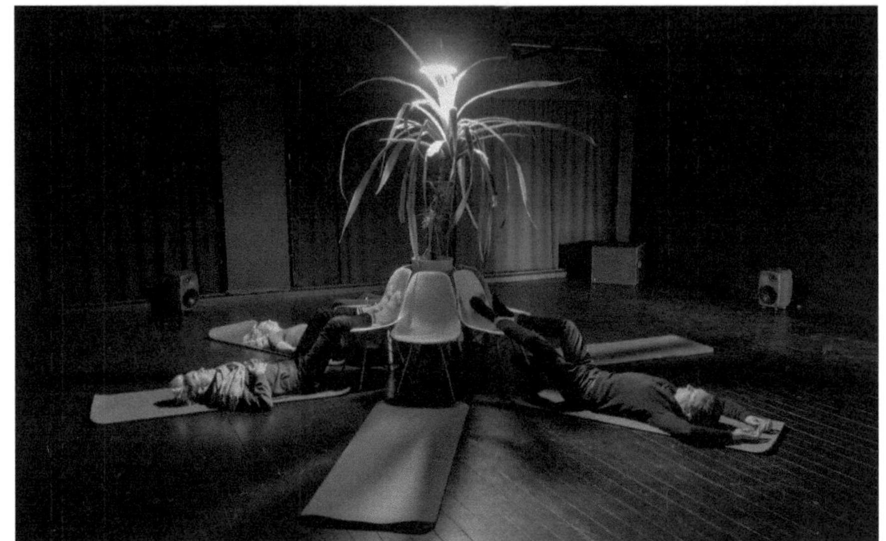

Photo: Terje Östling

FEELERS

Sound installation by Julia Giertz (sound) and Lisa Nyberg (text and voice), approx. 20 minutes loop. Produced for INTONAL experimental sound festival at Inter Arts Center, Malmö, May 2018
Available at: http://www.lisanyberg.net/feelers/

Summary

In the installation the visitor is invited to lie down, immersed in a multi-channel sound scape, guided by a voice. "In this space we allow ourselves to become with the deep network of the cephalopod molluscs, such as octopuses, cuttlefish and squids. The body of the cephalopod is tender and pliant. Their highly decentralized nervous system re-locates brainpower throughout the body, into a myriad of local neural networks – feelers of extreme sensibility. In a collective effort to anticipate the future, we are learning to stay with the trouble, of living and dying, together on this damaged earth. We invite you to dissolve and de-normalize in a space of speculative fabulation, feminist mythology, immersive audio and sound as touch. Our bodies are activated as we expand into softness."

Manuscript
Sound loop in six chapters, 22 minutes

We invite you to a space of meditation. You can enter at any time and stay as long as you like.

Please take off your shoes and leave them, with any bag, on the shelf just inside the door. Turn off your phone.

There are six meditation mats in the room. Lie down on a mat with your feet up on the chair. You can use your jacket or sweater as a pillow or as a blanket, or to support your knees. You can keep your eyes open or closed. We encourage you to engage with this work in whichever way you feel able to. You will not have to lie completely still, and do not worry if you should drift off or fall asleep.

Trigger warnings: this meditation makes references to deep water, inner organs, old wounds and shape shifting and contains strong, vibrating bass sounds. Remember – you can leave at any time.
Please close the door after entering.

0.
we invite you to submerge
into the deep
to connect with the deep network
of the cephalopod molluscs

we ask for you to find
a radical openness
to let yourself be changed
by this encounter
let yourself overflow and connect
with other, as other
to let your most, moist inner sensations out
and become
become with
the cephalopod

1.
feel the palm of your left hand
and the palm of your right hand
and bring them up towards your face
to cover your eyes
the heel of your palm
resting on the cheekbones
fingers on the forehead
a pocket of air between your palms and your eye balls
dark and safe

push lightly down on the bones surrounding the eye socket
cheekbones, brows and forehead
let your eyeballs fall back
into your head
merging in darkness
back into the brain

you can keep your hands in this position, or let them go,
however you feel comfortable
but keep your eyes closed for a while

guide your sight towards your ears
let them be your new eyes
big, round,
let your ears open
to an extended visual scope
let your eyes encompass all directions
a complex, global vision
a retina open to the full range of light vibrations
purple, blue, white, red

your new eyes receive input from all around
loads of information to process
do not bother to understand
to make sense

to sort it out
befriend the feeling of overload and uncertainty
receive
take your time
and trust, your pupils will always find their horizon

2.
let yourself fall
back into the future
your body re-orienting itself
by the sounds

3.
feel your bones
how they respond to vibrations
in your hips, back, shoulders, arms, legs
loosening the joints,
from ligaments, muscles
vibrating at your core

let go of bone structure
to embrace a soft, pliant, flexible body
letting the marrow
dissolve
into soft tissue
bones merge
into muscles and fluids
expand into softness

trust in your body's ability
to hold itself
boneless
spineless
extended

4.
feel your lips
their precise sense of touch
and taste
gate keepers of the inside to outside
judging over good and bad

your tongue
this independent muscle
movable in three dimensions
curling up or stretching out
sense texture and taste in millions of taste buds
comprehending in beautiful, advanced patterns

follow your nervous system
from the tip of your tongue
centre of tongue
back of the tongue
down your throat
following the food pipe
down your stomach
through the small intestine
colon
rectum
to the intelligent anus

from this alignment
find a focus point
a bundle of nerves
deep in your gut
close to where your spine has been
from this place
your new limb will take form
it will grow out of you
a new organ of touch
a feeler

5.
this
is where the hard work begins
we ask you to tap into the vulnerability
of living
and dying
together on this damaged earth

to bare your wounds
in this salty sea
and let your scars soften
for a chance
to build new tissue

use your body's deep memory
as the rooted system
for a new limb to take form
a new, boneless arm
a feeler
extended
with the wisdom
that comes from being hurt

this new tissue
is soft and pink
raw and sensitive
alive

absorb nutrition
brought to you by deep sea currents
from the death and decomposition
of unnamed relatives
connecting across the continental rift
you share this nourishing womb
with most life
on this earth

let your new feeler grow
with the empathic pattern
that comes from knowing each other
in vulnerability
and pain
the necessary connection
of living
body-to-body

6.
as your grow into the world
lend yourself to the thick, fluid, slow moving tissue
grow with the resilience of a rubbery, bouncy texture
find protection in a tough and smooth surface,
you are all these things

your feeler
acts independently from central control
with it, you can feel your way around
you can grip and hold
walk and swim
it is strong, in sensitivity
unconstrained
muscle
acting from your deepest resolve and courage

embrace the joy
of your extensible glory
your new body-form
unimaginable
incredible
awesome
ready

Photo: Lisa Nyberg

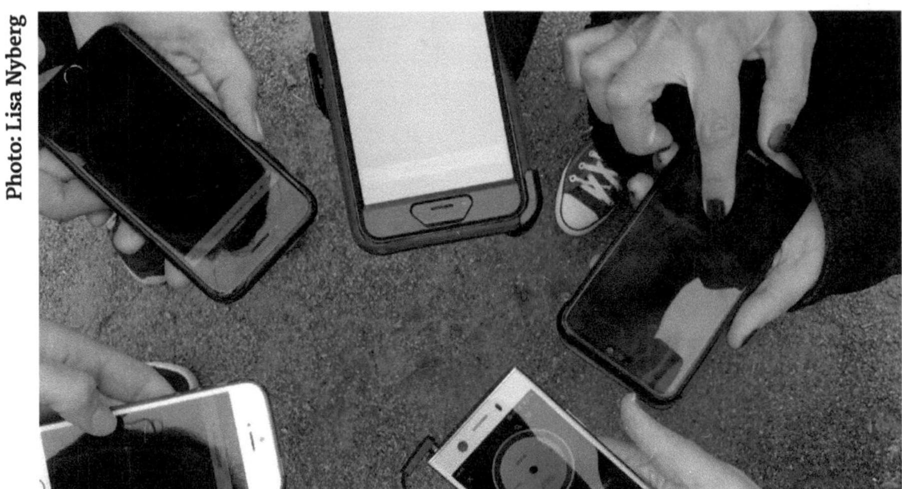

ANTIFASCISTISK GATUMEDITATION – DIN NÄRVARO ÄR EN KÄRLEKSHANDLING

Published online, May 1st 2019. Collective listening events in Malmö and Stockholm on May 1st 2019 and May 1st 2020. Presented as part of Queer Treasure Quest, Malmö, 2021

Text and sound: Lisa Nyberg
Sound and text: Julia Giertz
Available at: http://www.lisanyberg.net /antifascistisk-gatumeditation-antifascist-street-meditation/
https://soundcloud.com/junkotherose/antifascistisk-gatumeditation

Summary

"We would like to invite you to an anti-fascist street meditation. This is a walking meditation that takes about 15 minutes. You can listen to it on your way home from work, on the bus, on a walk on your block, alone or together with friends. The meditation aims at supporting our coping mechanisms in face of rising fascism in Sweden, and provides an exercise in bringing attention to your inner strength as well as our collective power. This is a practice in readiness. Your presence is an act of love."

Manuscript

Vi vill välkomna dig till en meditation i antifascistisk beredskap. Det här är en gående meditation på ca 15 minuter. Du kan lyssna på den när du går till bussen eller hem från jobbet, på en promenad i dina kvarter, genom byn, själv eller tillsammans med vänner. Meditationen är tänkt som ett stöd i att mota bort paniken vid tanken på fascismens framfart i Sverige, och en övning i att rikta uppmärksamhet mot din inneboende motståndskraft, såväl som vår kollektiva styrka. Det här är en övning i beredskap.

Din närvaro är en kärlekshandling.

Låt oss börja.
Gå, alldeles som vanligt.
Du kan låta händerna vila i fickorna på jackan,
eller släppa ner dina armar att svinga vid sidorna
med öppna, avslappnade händer.
Försök hitta ett sätt där dina axlar kan slappna av.
Ta några djupa andetag.
Fyll lungorna och magen.
Se om du kan förlänga din utandning med några sekunder.
Låt ansiktet slappna av, släpp trycket i käkarna,
kring munnen och ögonen.
Gäspa om du känner för det.
Släpp uppmärksamheten på människor
i din omgivning.
Du behöver inte bry dig om dem, inte le, inte hälsa.
Du tar en paus och skiftar fokus.

1.
Du går på gatan
genom dina kvarter
in mot centrum
eller på väg hem
Eller, du går på byn
på gågatan
förbi torget

eller mellan husen
i villakvarteret
Gatorna är bekanta
husen
gatstenarna
den där sprickan i asfalten
det här är hemma för dig
det har varit det ett tag

Du följer trottoaren och känner gatans lukter
en bris av bekanta dofter
luften som svalkar mot ansiktet
ljud når dig från öppna fönster
människors röster, barn som leker
bilar som drar förbi
ljudet av dina egna skor mot marken

2.
Gatan fylls sakta av människor
några bekanta
andra okända

du betraktar dem
undrande:
Vem sprider falsk information i nätets chattrum
och vem blåser upp det på tidningens ledarsida?
Vem ropar glåpord åt barn och drar slöjor av kvinnor på gatan?
Vem är det som röstar på ett rasistiskt, fascistiskt parti?
Vem lägger motioner om tiggeriförbud och vem
startar bränder på flyktingförläggningar?
Vem godkänner utökade gränskontroller och vem gör människor rättslösa?
Vem håller batongen och vem ger ordern?
Vem smyger om natten med lasersikte?
Vem tjänar pengar på allt detta systematiska våld?
Vem är bara aningslös och vem är nöjd med att se
åt andra hållet?

Du ser dig omkring
och räknar
bland alla kroppar
rasister
fascister
personer villiga att spela med människors värde
för en illusion av trygghet
Redo att sortera bort
dig och dina vänner
Frånta er era rättigheter
till plats, till liv
Frånta er er mänsklighet
med våld

3.
Din kropp svarar på hotet
Det börjar som ett pirr
djupt inne i dina handflator
vibrationer som strömmar ut i fingrarna
och något rör sig
drar ihop sig
i magen
Du fortsätter andas
djupa andetag
Du underskattar inte hotet
men du behåller ditt lugn
och fokuserar på det som händer
inuti

En låga
som bränner
i maggropen
som brinner
i mitten av din kropp
Du, är inte rädd för elden
den värmer dig
inifrån

den skyddar dig
från att bli kall och stel
från att bli obrydd, apatisk, eller förlamad av rädsla
Så du eldar på
ger bränsle
till elden
ger den syre
vid varje andetag
och känner värmen från lågan
het och klar
i mitten av ditt inre

Du går stadigt framåt
fötterna fäster bra i marken
Du känner kontakt
du är jordad
balanserad
orubblig
marken möter upp
och skickar kraft upp genom benen
för varje steg känner du styrkan
i höfterna, i ryggen, i nacken

Du släpper ner axlarna
och armarna
dina händer tunga och starka vid sidorna
Du känner dina handflator och fingrar
öppnar och stänger dem
öppnar
De är redo
att fånga, hålla, skydda,
mota bort, knuffa, slå om det behövs

Du andas djupt och stadigt
ner i magen
syresätter lågan som brinner
den skiftar färg

och intensitet
vid varje andetag

4.
Du tillåter dig att vara mjuk och mottaglig
att hålla blicken öppen
och letar efter ögonkontakt
letar efter varma ögon
som möter en tyst överenskommelse i din blick
Du skickar ut signaler
vibrationer
till de dina
Du känner in energin
från varma kroppar
som svarar
tills du vet
med hela din kropp
att vi är många
redo
att sluta upp

Du tillåter dig att lita till andra
kända och okända
att luta dig mot vår kollektiva styrka

5.
Vi riktar vår uppmärksamhet
mot de av oss som är mest utsatta
Det är där våldet tar sikte
alltid på de mest utsatta
de systematiskt åtsatta
på de som kämpat hårdast
på ögonblick av utmattning
och skyddslöshet
Vi samlas till en mur
ett skydd

av tusen ryggar
stadiga fötter
som håller plats
för varandra
håller plats
för våra svagheter
håller plats
för våra olikheter
våra kroppar
våra grannar
våra barn
våra liv

Vi tar oss fram på gatan
tillsammans
Vi roterar
så alla får vila
När du går hem
håller andra plats åt dig
tills du är beredd
att ta över igen

Här
närvarande
redo

Vi håller den här platsen
för varandra

MALMÖ KONSTVERKSTAD

Malmö Konstverkstad was a one-year program that combined studies to prepare for higher education with arts education. Two days a week the focus was on socially engaged art and contemporary creative practises. The program started from the basic assumption that every student is an artist, and that lived experience from outside of main sociality is an asset. By combining making art with encountering art, meeting different art professionals and talking to artists and other creative change makers, the program offered an understanding of the context in which art is produced and presented, as well as how art plays a role in the history and the direction of our society.

In February 2017 the participants of Malmö Konstverkstad compiled the exhibition The War with Myself, with works from the collection of Malmö Art Museum. The students got a backstage pass to the museum, with a chance to encounter the art collection and the various professionals that work with it. The idea was to give the participants an insight into a context where art is produced, collected and shown. By making an exhibition with art works from the collection, the participants got the opportunity to express themselves through the means of curating. A special focus was put on developing a common theme that was urgent and personal to the participants, and how to formulate texts that presented the works in ways they could relate to.

The War with Myself told a story of our inner struggles to battle anxiety, depression and addiction. Among the exhibiting artists were Elin Behrens, Nathalie Djurberg, Sirous Namazi, Leif Holmstrand, Vassil Simittchiev and Annika von Hausswolff.

The exhibition was compiled by the participants of Malmö Konstverkstad: Sherin Alabtah, Sofia Brodén, I was the head teacher and coordinator of the program, which was initiated by me and Folkrörelsernas Konstfrämjande, in collaboration with Malmö Folkhögskola and Malmö Konstmuseum. The initiative was part of a larger effort to make the art world more democratic and relevant to our times, by giving access to art education to groups in our society that are under-represented in our art institutions.

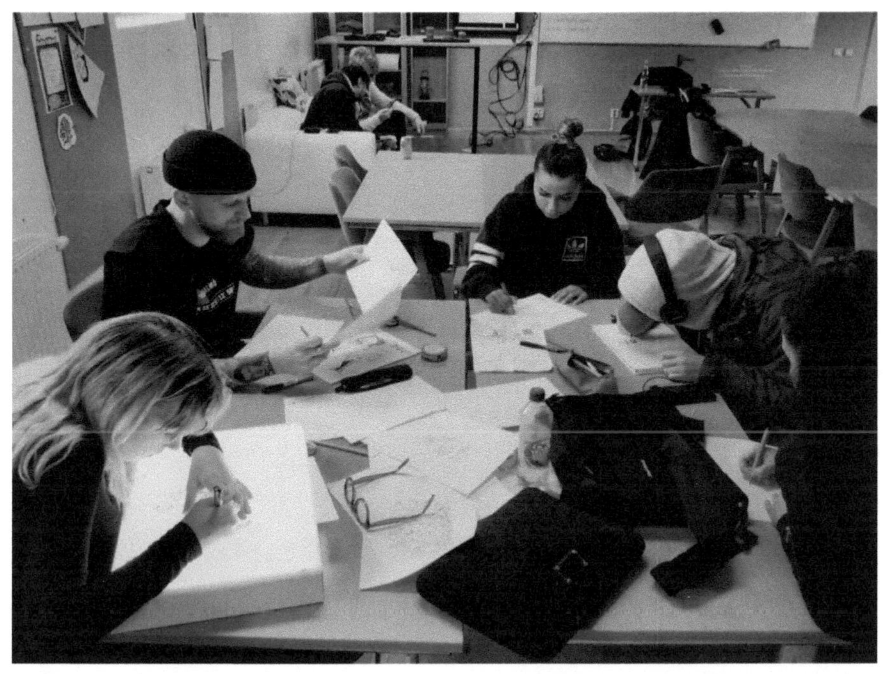

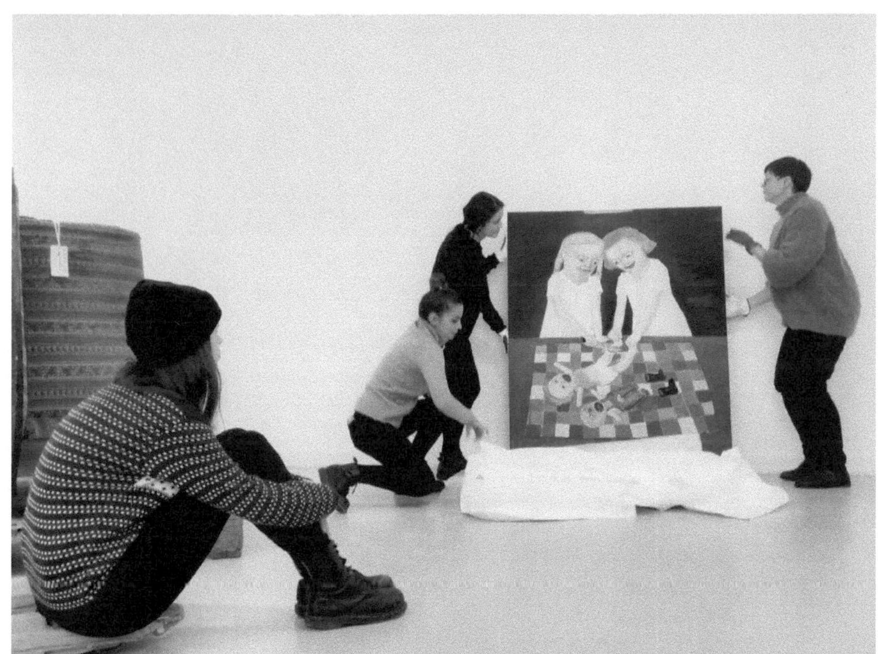

Photo: Lisa Nyberg